# Gu

CW00689829

September–December 2014

*Commissioned by* **David Spriggs;** *Edited by* **Lisa Cherrett**

Guidelines © BRF 2014
**The Bible Reading Fellowship**
15 The Chambers, Vineyard, Abingdon OX14 3FE
Tel: 01865 319700; Fax: 01865 319701
E-mail: enquiries@brf.org.uk; Websites: www.brf.org.uk; www.biblereadingnotes.org.uk

ISBN 978 0 85746 042 4

Distributed in Australia by Mediacom Education Inc., PO Box 610, Unley, SA 5061.
Tel: 1800 811 311; Fax: 08 8297 8719;
E-mail: admin@mediacom.org.au
Available also from all good Christian bookshops in Australia.
For individual and group subscriptions in Australia:
Mrs Rosemary Morrall, PO Box W35, Wanniassa, ACT 2903.

Distributed in New Zealand by Scripture Union Wholesale, PO Box 760, Wellington
Tel: 04 385 0421; Fax: 04 384 3990; E-mail: suwholesale@clear.net.nz

Publications distributed to more than 60 countries

## Acknowledgments

Printed by Gutenberg Press, Tarxien, Malta.

# Suggestions for using *Guidelines*

Set aside a regular time and place, if possible, when you can read and pray undisturbed. Before you begin, take time to be still and, if you find it helpful, use the BRF prayer.

In *Guidelines*, the introductory section provides context for the passages or themes to be studied, while the units of comment can be used daily, weekly, or whatever best fits your timetable. You will need a Bible (more than one if you want to compare different translations) as Bible passages are not included. At the end of each week is a 'Guidelines' section, offering further thoughts about, or practical application of what you have been studying.

Occasionally, you may read something in *Guidelines* that you find particularly challenging, even uncomfortable. This is inevitable in a series of notes which draws on a wide spectrum of contributors, and doesn't believe in ducking difficult issues. Indeed, we believe that *Guidelines* readers much prefer thought-provoking material to a bland diet that only confirms what they already think.

If you do disagree with a contributor, you may find it helpful to go through these three steps. First, think about why you feel uncomfortable. Perhaps this is an idea that is new to you, or you are not happy at the way something has been expressed. Or there may be something more substantial—you may feel that the writer is guilty of sweeping generalisation, factual error, theological or ethical misjudgment. Second, pray that God would use this disagreement to teach you more about his word and about yourself. Third, think about what you will do as a result of the disagreement. You might resolve to find out more about the issue, or write to the contributor or the editors of *Guidelines*.

To send feedback, you may email or write to BRF at the addresses shown opposite. If you would like your comment to be included on our website, please email connect@brf.org.uk. You can also Tweet to @brfonline, using the hashtag #brfconnect.

# Writers in this issue

**Walter Moberly** is a Professor in the Department of Theology and Religion at Durham University. He is the proud husband of Jenny, the doting father of John-Paul and Rachel, and a long-suffering supporter of Sunderland AFC.

**Rachel Jordan** is the National Adviser for Mission and Evangelism for the Church of England. She works with the Diocesan Missioners and many other agencies who see themselves as part of a network within the church with a special calling for mission and evangelism.

**Brian Howell** is Tutor in Old Testament on the West of England Ministerial Training Course at Redcliffe College, Gloucester.

**Joanna Collicutt**, an Anglican priest, is a lecturer in Psychology and Spirituality at Ripon College Cuddesdon, Oxford, as well as Oxford Diocesan Advisor for Spiritual Care for Older People. She is a chartered clinical psychologist.

**Nigel G. Wright** was Principal of Spurgeon's College from 2000 to 2013 and is a former President of the Baptist Union of Great Britain. He has written *Jesus Christ—the Alpha and the Omega* for BRF (2010).

**Hugh Williamson** is the Regius Professor of Hebrew at Oxford University. He has written extensively on the books of Chronicles, Ezra and Nehemiah, and Isaiah, including *Variations on a Theme: King, Messiah and Servant in the Book of Isaiah* (Paternoster, 1988).

**Paul Moore** is Vicar of St Wilfrid's Church, Cowplain, an Anglican church near Portsmouth, and a member of the team that launched the first Messy Church in 2004.

**David Spriggs** is a Baptist minister who has worked for the last 15 years with Bible Society, helping the churches and Higher Education to engage more fruitfully with the Bible.

**Lisa Cherrett** is BRF's Project Editor and Managing Editor for the Bible reading notes. She is also a contributor to *Quiet Spaces*, BRF's prayer and spirituality resource.

**Stuart Murray Williams** works under the auspices of the Anabaptist Network as a trainer and consultant, with particular interest in urban mission, church planting and emerging forms of church.

# The Editor writes...

Welcome to this autumn edition of *Guidelines*. We start with dark days for Judah and Jerusalem as the Babylonian exile looms ever nearer, seen through the eyes, words and heartache of the prophet Jeremiah. Under the expertise of Walter Moberly we enter into Jeremiah's world and hear again the challenge of living for God in a world that is seeking easy solutions and deceiving itself about the dangers.

We end 2014 and peep into 2015 in the company of 1 Peter. Stuart Murray Williams helps us to see the parallels between the position of God's people then and now, in exile, and the stimulation of a Christ-centred faith and life, thus opening up the missional value of this text for ourselves today.

In between we have a host of stimulating contributions. Rachel Jordan offers some excellent reflections on harvest for HOPE 2014. Brian Howell invites us to journey through the first half of Exodus, a foundational text for God's people, taking us on a pilgrimage from despair to deliverance and establishment.

Joanna Collicutt then uses her dual competence in psychology and theology to help us to think more biblically about appreciating old age and older people, and Nigel Wright continues his study of Matthew's Gospel. Chapters 11—14 include insights about John the Baptist in prison and about the nature of Jesus as well as many of his parables.

Isaiah 49—55 are vibrant chapters of promise and hope from God, but embedded in them is that most powerful image of the 'suffering servant', especially in chapter 53. Hugh helps us to see what these chapters would have meant in their historical context, without losing sight of the need to integrate this with our understanding of Jesus. Next, Paul Moore challenges us to explore the community dimensions of discipleship, bringing us insights from both Old and New Testaments.

Finally, Lisa Cherrett and I offer some material to help us through Advent to Christmas. I focus on one of the great prophetic passages from the early chapters of Isaiah, seeking to engage with aspects of the life of Jesus that correspond to Isaiah's insights. Lisa helps us journey to Bethlehem to see the child who is born, as we explore passages that focus on Mary, the mother of Jesus.

These various readings are united by an insistence that we face up to the often difficult aspects of human life with the divine hope and resources that come from God.

*David Spriggs*

# The BRF Prayer

Almighty God,
you have taught us that your word is a lamp for our
feet and a light for our path. Help us, and all who
prayerfully read your word, to deepen our
fellowship with you and with each other through your love.
And in so doing may we come to know you more fully,
love you more truly, and follow more faithfully in
the steps of your son Jesus Christ, who lives and
reigns with you and the Holy Spirit,
one God for evermore. Amen.

# A Prayer for Remembrance

Heavenly Father, we commit ourselves to work in
penitence and faith for reconciliation between the
nations, that all people may, together, live in
freedom, justice and peace. We pray for all who
in bereavement, disability and pain continue to
suffer the consequences of fighting and terror.
We remember with thanksgiving and sorrow those
whose lives, in world wars and conflicts past and
present, have been given and taken away.

FROM AN ORDER OF SERVICE FOR REMEMBRANCE SUNDAY,
CHURCHES TOGETHER IN BRITAIN AND IRELAND 2005

# Jeremiah

Jeremiah is the longest book of Hebrew prophecy. It is difficult partly because the sequence of material can be hard to follow. The speaking voice often changes, and its identity is not always clear; poetry alternates with prose, with biographical snippets interspersed; some passages are dated but not in chronological sequence. There is no obvious reason for all of these difficulties. Scholarly literature abounds with complex hypotheses about differing contributors to the writing of the book as a way of trying to account for some of these difficulties. Here I will simply take the liberty of selectively moving to and fro within the book to try to clarify certain significant issues.

The book is difficult also because much of its content speaks of God's judgement on human faithlessness, as a result of which disaster becomes increasingly inescapable. Such content is not exactly congenial.

The book is accessible, however, because it contains astonishingly vivid narratives about Jeremiah's life as a prophet in Jerusalem. We get a sense of factions, intrigue, *realpolitik* and the ruthless pressure that can be brought to bear upon someone who says things that other people do not want to hear. Jeremiah's own voice speaks unforgettably in anguish and perplexity.

The picture of God's ways with the world that emerges from this book is neither easy nor comfortable. Nonetheless, an important paradox about the book of Jeremiah is that a prophet to whom most people refused to listen during his lifetime has been preserved as a voice and a life to whom all generations should attend.

In the first week we will consider the nature of Jeremiah's prophetic language and ministry. God's word comes in human words, closely related to the particularities of human life, and it comes with a power to change and direct lives and nations. Yet the message is response-seeking and its outworking is contingent upon how people respond to it, as God, though sovereign in power, is also responsive towards those he has made.

In week 2, we will consider some of the specific challenges and opposition that Jeremiah met—his interactions with the two kings Jehoiakim and Zedekiah, whose reigns identify the context of most of his ministry (1:3), and his interactions with other contemporary prophets, especially Hananiah. Strong antagonism remained the dominant response to Jeremiah's life and words and, in some ways, posterity has not been kinder. Jeremiah has become proverbial as a misery-guts and a kill-joy, the epitome of someone who casts a pall over life by speaking only of doom and gloom.

So what did his prophetic ministry mean for Jeremiah himself, and in what way, if any, is there real hope and joy in his life and message? This will be the general angle of approach in our last week of readings as we consider an Old Testament form of the way of the cross.

Quotations are taken from the New Revised Standard Version.

# 1 Setting the scene

Jeremiah 1:1–3

This short introduction merits a little lingering. First, it vividly portrays the basic nature of Hebrew prophecy: 'The words of Jeremiah… to whom the word of the LORD came'. There are human words and a divine word. The two are simply juxtaposed, with no explanation of how they relate (although, as the book proceeds, we will receive a fuller picture of what is involved). The claim that both realities, divine and human, are involved is at the heart of the biblical concept of revelation. To acknowledge this claim and take it seriously is to read and respond in faith.

The Old Testament has no hesitation in portraying God as speaking in ordinary language. Yet theologians have always wanted to balance positive analogy (God speaks as we speak) with negative analogy (God is not like us and transcends all human categories). Although, in the book of Jeremiah as a whole, there is no absolute distinction between human words as plural and the divine word as singular, the wording here can be seen as anticipating what became a regular idiomatic distinction, and recognition of difference, in Christian theology: 'God's *word* in human *words*'.

Second, a precise context is given for Jeremiah's ministry. In modern chronology, Josiah's 13th year was 627BC, while Zedekiah's eleventh year was 587BC, so a 40-year ministry for Jeremiah is envisaged, which might perhaps suggest an analogy with Moses. Nonetheless, despite the reference to Josiah's reign, almost all the specifically dated material in the book is dated to the reigns of Jehoiakim (609–598) and Zedekiah

(597–587). Thus Jeremiah's ministry is located in the final years of the kingdom of Judah and its capital Jerusalem, until Judah was overcome by Babylon and many of its people were taken into exile. In fact, Jeremiah's ministry continued for a short while after Jerusalem was captured (see chs. 40—44), but Jerusalem's fall clearly constitutes its climax.

Although people sometimes speak of 'timeless truths' as constituting the heart of faith in God, such an expression would find no place in the book of Jeremiah. Here God's truth is expressed through a particular person, in a particular place, at a particular time—as it was also in and through Jesus, 'crucified under Pontius Pilate'. Although the content is of enduring significance, its particular colouring is intrinsic to it, and we need to hold the two together.

# 2 God calls Jeremiah

Jeremiah 1:4–10

Jeremiah tells of his call to be 'a prophet to the nations' (v. 5b). This is remarkable not least because, for almost all his ministry, he was located in or around Jerusalem. Admittedly, there is a group of oracles to other nations, from Egypt to Babylon, located at the end of the book (chs. 46—51), but these hardly seem to define Jeremiah's prophetic ministry. The point may be that the content of his message—the concerns of the moral God for integrity and justice, for repentance and faithfulness—matters not only for the people of Judah but also for other nations.

God carefully prefaces the commission with words that undergird it (v. 5a). Although the language used has often encouraged readers to speculate about 'predestination', to think about such an issue here is to misread through abstracting the words from their context. The words are not an intellectual puzzle but an assurance that God knows what he is doing in commissioning Jeremiah: being a prophet is what he is made for, and if he fulfils this role he will realise his true being.

Perhaps unsurprisingly, Jeremiah feels that such a responsibility is too much for him; he is hardly up to it (v. 6). The LORD takes this response seriously, meeting it with words of reassurance: when Jeremiah goes, the LORD will go with him and will protect him (vv. 7–8). Moreover, the LORD symbolically enacts and enables Jeremiah's prophetic speech by touching his mouth and giving him words to say (vv. 9–10).

Astonishingly, Jeremiah, a figure with no political or military status, is appointed over nations, both to pull them down and to build them up. What kind of authority and power is this? When Elijah was taken up to heaven, Elisha exclaimed, 'Father! Father! The chariots of Israel and its horsemen!' (2 Kings 2:12), which apparently means that Elisha saw Elijah's as Israel's true strength, for in what Elijah said and did, God's presence and power were made known. So too Jeremiah depicts God's word as 'a hammer that breaks a rock in pieces' (Jer. 23:29). Jeremiah's power (and Hebrew prophecy's enduring contribution to the world) is moral and spiritual—that which burns the heart, shakes the mind and changes how people live and what they live for.

## 3 How prophetic speech 'works'

Jeremiah 18:1–12

We jump ahead in the book, because what is said in the potter's house develops and clarifies the nature of Jeremiah's commission in 1:10.

Initially, Jeremiah is told to go to the potter because the potter's workshop will be the appropriate context for what the LORD will say (vv. 1–4). The message begins by drawing a straightforward analogy: as clay in the potter's hands, so is Israel in God's hands (vv. 5–6). The imagery is suggestive of divine power, for a potter can do anything he wants with clay. So God can, in principle, make, remake or discard his people as he wills.

But the sequel is surprising. The message about God's power over Israel shifts into a general point about God addressing nations or kingdoms (vv. 7–10). This makes clear that what applies to Israel applies to other nations and vice versa. It also clarifies the way Jeremiah's speaking for God 'works'. On the one hand, a pronouncement of judgement and disaster can be averted through repentance (vv. 7–8). On the other hand, a promise of good can be forfeited through complacency and corruption (vv. 9–10). This shows two things about prophetic speech: first, it is response-seeking, and second, its outworking is dependent upon the response that is given. The most famous biblical example is seen in Jonah's words at Nineveh, where a seemingly categorical message of disaster evokes a turning to God, such that God does not, after all, bring the disaster (see Jonah 3:4–10, where the wording of verse 10 evokes Jeremiah 18:8). This means also that the way people act and react to a prophet matters and makes a difference to the way God will act. The Hebrew word in 18:8 and 10 that is translated 'change my mind' or 'relent' is making a point not about divine psychology but about divine relationality and responsiveness. In life generally, warnings and invitations work this way: they are relational and try to restore or enhance relationships.

In context, this is also a striking interpretation of the total power that God has, like a potter with clay: God's power is not used arbitrarily but morally and responsively. Sadly, Jeremiah's immediate audience couldn't care less (vv. 11–12).

# 4  Jeremiah's temple sermon

Jeremiah 7:1–15

The temple in Jerusalem was the symbolic heart of the kingdom of Judah. Here the LORD was specially present with his people (1 Kings 8:10–13) and here Israel could celebrate the LORD's promised protection of his people (Psalms 46; 48). Yet we saw in Jeremiah 18:9–10 that divine promises are response-seeking and contingent in their outworking. What if the right response is not given?

Jeremiah is to position himself in the place of maximum impact (vv. 1–2), with two prime things to say: first, a challenge to moral reformation as the basis for security (vv. 3, 5–7), and, second, a warning against false confidence in words separated from appropriate actions (vv. 48–11).

The challenge to 'amend' is given characteristic content in terms of acting with integrity, especially towards the marginal in society—that is, those of whom one could most easily take advantage (vv. 5–6). If justice is done here, then it will be done elsewhere too. If the Judahites do thus change their ways, God will respond by letting the people remain in their homeland (vv. 3, 7). (The NRSV margin, 'I will let you dwell', is preferable to the text 'let me dwell' in verses 3 and 7; the issue is not God's possible departure from the temple, as in Ezekiel 8—11, but rather whether the people can escape exile as a consequence of their corruption, as is specified in Jeremiah 7:15.)

Jeremiah also warns the people not to trust in 'deceptive words' (vv. 4, 8). Yet since the building they are all standing at *is* the temple of the LORD, why is something factually true said to be deceptive? The meaning of the people's words in verse 4 is clarified by their further words in verse 10: 'we are safe'. Clearly they were appealing to the temple as guaranteeing God's protection because of his presence. But Jeremiah tells the people that they cannot have it both ways: they cannot ignore God's moral will, as expressed in the ten commandments (v. 9), and still appeal to his presence and protection (v. 10). God's promises are to enable living rightly, and living corruptly may mean that the promise is forfeited.

There is a precedent for the warning about the Jerusalem temple in what happened to Shiloh (vv. 12–15), once the site of a temple but long since a heap of ruins (see 1 Samuel 3—4). If people are corrupt, God's presence is no assurance of safety.

# 5  Events surrounding the temple sermon

**Jeremiah 26**

If Jeremiah 7:1–15 concentrates on Jeremiah's words in his temple sermon, with only a minimal narrative setting (7:1–2), the opposite is true in Jeremiah 26. Here Jeremiah's message of warning and challenge is briefly summarised (vv. 1–6), and the focus is on the response to what he says.

Initially the temple clergy close in on Jeremiah, and the crowd with them (vv. 7–9). They accuse Jeremiah of, in effect, treason, a supreme offence that merits the death penalty. If the temple is to be a ruin and its people in exile, that will be because their enemies have conquered them, and they hear Jeremiah as advocating this outcome.

However, the uproar being caused by the response to Jeremiah alerts officials in the nearby palace, and they come quickly to prevent a lynching and ensure some kind of legal process (v. 10). So the clergy make a formal accusation, trying to persuade both crowd and officials of their case (v. 11). Jeremiah's defence is to point strikingly to the content of his message. His warning must speak for itself; if it does not persuade them that he is not treacherous, nothing else will (vv. 12–15). The officials take his point, as does also the crowd (v. 16).

Now other people ('elders') appear, and they appeal to the precedent of Micah (vv. 18–19), which we will consider in detail tomorrow. For the present we may simply note that they conclude by warning that to respond hard-heartedly to Jeremiah may be disastrous.

The narrative continues with an account of another prophet, Uriah, and it is not clear whether these words are spoken by the elders or the narrator (vv. 20–23). Indeed, it is not obvious why Uriah's story is told at all. Maybe Uriah's fearfulness contrasts with Jeremiah's courage; maybe it reminds us that death threats against prophets were not idle words.

Either way, the account ends with decisive action on the part of Ahikam, clearly one of the officials (v. 24). His father, Shaphan, was also a significant official under Josiah, in the context of Josiah's famous discovery of the book of the law and subsequent reform (2 Kings 22). Father and son alike appear to have been faithful to the LORD. For Jeremiah, it means that the LORD's initial promise of deliverance (1:8) is realised through a faithful human agent.

# 6 Jeremiah and Micah

Jeremiah 26:18–19; Micah 3:9–12

The elders who intervene in the controversy around Jeremiah in the temple area appeal to the precedent of a prophet named Micah—who is, in fact, the canonical Micah. They cite Micah 3:12 verbatim. Micah, a century previously, also pronounced the destruction of Jerusalem and its temple.

The elders' appeal is rich in implication. Micah's words in their immediate context challenge the corrupt rulers of Jerusalem for their violence and injustice (Micah 3:9–10). Specifically, he charges that those in authority, both secular and spiritual, are venal: all they say and do has its price (3:11a). Yet at the same time they appeal to the LORD's presence in the temple and his corresponding protection of his people (3:11b). This combination of corruption with complacency, of assuming that they can ignore God's will and yet claim his protection, is what will bring disaster ('therefore because of you', Micah 3:12a): the LORD's presence will bring the opposite of what they expect (3:12b).

There is thus a strong parallel between the temple sermons of Jeremiah (7:1–15) and that of Micah (3:9–12). In each context the people are quoted as appealing to the LORD's protection ('We are safe', Jeremiah 7:10; 'No harm shall come upon us', Micah 3:11) while being equally heedless of God's moral will. There is therefore good precedent for what Jeremiah has said.

Further, the elders are concerned with the response that Micah's words evoked. Although the temple was still standing a century after he had spoken of its destruction, this does not show that Micah was mistaken. Rather, his words achieved their purpose. They moved Hezekiah to repentance, such that the LORD responded mercifully (Jeremiah 26:19, compare 18:8). Thus Micah's words were response-seeking, and their outcome was dependent on the response given—just as Jeremiah's words are (26:3). The true fulfilment of a prophetic warning of disaster is not that the disaster takes place, but that people turn to God and, in that turning, discover the mercy of God.

## Guidelines

We have seen a regular contrast between God's will and human will. God seeks obedient faithfulness on Jeremiah's part, despite his initially feeling overwhelmed. God seeks justice, integrity and openness to hear his voice, from a people who, even though nominally God's own people, are more inclined to self-seeking. Whatever else has changed since the world of Jeremiah, this conflict has not. If we hear God's voice in the words of Jeremiah, will we harden our hearts or not?

For Jeremiah, the people's heedless reliance on God's promises with respect to Jerusalem and the temple indicated a 'false faith'. Are there similar symbols and associated promises to which we, as Christians today, might give 'false faith'? What should we do about them?

Jeremiah was often called to stand against the leaders of his own day. What might be the issue where we are called to take a stand? What might be the price for doing so? Pray for people and organisations who are doing this. Uriah, with a similar message to Jeremiah's, was murdered, while Jeremiah was spared this fate. Reread the story in Jeremiah 26:20–23 and use it to prompt prayer for those who are in mortal danger today because of their faith.

# 1 Jeremiah faces King Jehoiakim (1)

Jeremiah 9:23–24; 22:13–19

At the heart of all that Jeremiah says is his vision of God. A succinct and justly famous summary of that vision is 9:23–24. Knowledge, strength and wealth are things to which people regularly appeal, on which they base themselves and where they seek to find value and meaning in their lives (v. 23), but Jeremiah relativises them all in relation to the surpassing worth of knowing the living God, the LORD (v. 24a; compare Paul's testimony about knowing this God in the person of Jesus Christ, Philippians 3:4–11). This God is known not in the abstract but in concrete practices that display his character (v. 24b); that is, knowing God means being willing to conform the way we live to God's priorities.

The trouble is, people with power often have other priorities. King Jehoiakim is a particular problem (22:13–19). Like many a despot, Jehoiakim is too concerned with a prestigious building project, something that sounds like a state-of-the-art royal palace, which he wants to get built at minimal cost to himself (vv. 13–14). Jeremiah scornfully asks whether this is what real kingship is about (v. 15a) and goes on to compare Jehoiakim with his father, Josiah. Josiah acted with justice and integrity as regularly and consistently as he ate and drank. This not only demonstrated true kingship but also showed what it means to know the LORD (vv. 15b–16). Josiah's life and priorities reflected God's life and priorities, and thus displayed the reality of God in the world (compare the similar understanding in 1 John 4:7–8). Tragically, his son's priorities are greed and the use of others for his purposes.

As a result Jeremiah offers a stark picture of Jehoiakim's funeral (vv. 18–19). Instead of its being a place and time of regular mourning, people will treat Jehoiakim as no more than a dead animal; because Jehoiakim has denied the humanity of others, others will deny his humanity. Human life is enriched when it displays God's qualities but it becomes nothing if it is lived by aggrandising oneself at the expense of others.

## 2 Jeremiah faces King Jehoiakim (2)

Jeremiah 36

Jeremiah has been banned from the temple precincts (v. 5), probably because of his temple sermon and its aftermath. Thus his message is written down, courtesy of Baruch, so that the word of God shall not be silenced but may still be available. It remains all-important that the people of Judah should hear it and turn to God and perhaps avert disaster (vv. 1–8). Baruch then reads out the message at the appropriate place and time (vv. 9–10). The initial response is similar to the response when the book of the law was found in the temple (2 Kings 22): the message is so important that those in authority need to know about it. Baruch is first summoned to a group of royal officials, who hear the words with dismay and feel that the king also must hear. However, since the king is Jehoiakim (v. 1), the officials rightly anticipate that Jeremiah's words will not be well received. (One wonders whether the scroll contained the material now in 22:13–19!) So they make sure that both Baruch and Jeremiah are out of harm's way (vv. 11–19).

What follows is a classic depiction of what the Old Testament means in saying that a person's 'heart is hardened'. Jehoiakim cares nothing for the content of the scroll or the scroll itself or the counsel of some of his vocal officials (vv. 20–25); he despises the warning about the king of Babylon bringing disaster to the land (v. 29). He thinks not of repentance but of revenge: how can he get hold of Jeremiah and Baruch and do to these troublesome and treacherous men what he did to Uriah (v. 26, compare 26:20–23)? But as at the temple sermon, so now too God's initial promise to protect Jeremiah (1:8) is enacted through human help.

Moreover, Jehoiakim cannot escape by burning the scroll. A new scroll renews the warning: the king's obduracy makes disaster for himself and others inevitable (vv. 27–32).

In this vivid narrative we have a rare account of the way prophecy could be written down and of what might happen to the scroll on which it was written. If we treasure the content of scripture, we should never forget the courage, both in writing and in preserving, that lies behind our safely bound volume.

# 3 Jeremiah faces other prophets (1)

Jeremiah 6:13–14; 14:1–16

A recurrent problem for Jeremiah, a thorn in his flesh, is opposition from other contemporary (mostly unnamed) prophets (6:13–14). Their message, also spoken in the LORD's name, differs fundamentally from Jeremiah's. From the outset, Jeremiah has warned the people of Judah of danger that threatens from the north (1:14–16), that is, the direction from which the Babylonians would approach Jerusalem (as distinct from the Egyptians, who would come from the south). Jeremiah sees this danger as expressing God's judgment on the faithlessness and corruption of his people, so that renewed turning to God offers the only hope. But other prophets say the opposite: 'Peace, peace'. This is presumably what people desperately wanted to hear—a reassurance that everything would be all right. However, it is mere wishful thinking and unreality, for 'there is no peace'. To Jeremiah's mind, the prophets who tell people what they want to hear are motivated by their hope to do well financially out of it (6:13); it is the easy way rather than the narrow gate (see Matthew 7:13–14).

The people's preference for these other prophets leads to a new problem: the time for change and repentance may pass. Although the response-seeking and contingent nature of prophecy is basic, it is also possible that judgment may become inevitable, in which case the only hope lies in going through it rather than averting it. Thus, in a time of devastating drought (14:1–6), we hear words of repentance that sound as though they are from the heart (vv. 7–9). Yet the divine response is brusque: the people have made their bed and now should lie in it (v. 10). Indeed, Jeremiah is told no longer to intercede, and now neither prayer nor fasting will avert the coming disaster (vv. 11–12). When Jeremiah cries out about the other prophets who have promised peace, the LORD dismisses all such words as deceptive self-will (vv. 13–14). Such prophets will share fully in the disaster whose coming they have denied (vv. 15–16).

Jeremiah's message of inescapable judgment is hard for many contemporary readers. Our instincts are for peace and for life going well; we generally prefer reassuring messages to unsettling challenges. But it was even harder for Jeremiah, as his vocation brought him no thanks from a people whose self-will was deeply engrained, but only hatred and suffering.

## 4  Jeremiah faces other prophets (2)

Jeremiah 28

The otherwise unnamed prophets who oppose Jeremiah have a concrete embodiment in the person of Hananiah. After the Babylonians' initial capture and plundering of Jerusalem in 597BC, Hananiah still has a message of 'Peace, peace'—but it now promises the imminent restoration of plunder and exiles because the power of Babylon will be overthrown (vv. 1–5). Moreover, Hananiah chooses to make this pronouncement as a deliberate confrontation with Jeremiah in the most symbolic public space, the temple precincts, where there would also be a guaranteed large audience (vv. 1, 6).

How best should Jeremiah respond? Initially he opts for irony (vv. 6–9). He has no objection at all to the LORD's restoring plunder and exiles—indeed, let it be! The problem, though, is that wanting something to be true does not make it true. This means that we need to be suspicious of those who say what people want to hear; we should reserve judgment until we have good reason to believe them.

Hananiah decides that the most impressive and persuasive way to back up his words and confute Jeremiah is to carry out a symbolic action, of the sort that prophets often carried out (compare Hosea 1:2–5; 1 Kings 22:11). Jeremiah has been performing his own symbolic action by carrying a yoke on his neck as a symbol of Babylon's dominion (Jeremiah 27:1–12), so Hananiah removes and breaks the yoke, as symbolic of the imminent end of Babylonian power (28:10–11).

Jeremiah's response of quietly going his way (v. 11) has puzzled some readers. Does it mean that that he was at a loss for what to say, or even that he might have thought Hananiah was right? It is most likely that he simply sees no point in a slanging match. He has consistently spoken of the inevitability of Babylonian dominion and, in a sense, there is nothing further for him to say. If onlookers interpret his silence as meaning that Hananiah has 'won', then that must just be endured. If people will not hear him, they will not hear him.

Later, however, in private, Jeremiah confronts Hananiah and tells him that he has done the worst thing a prophet could—make people 'trust in a lie' (v. 15); that is, people have been deceived into complacency instead of truly turning to God (compare 7:4, 8). Tragically, the wages of this sin is death (vv. 16–17).

# 5 Jeremiah faces King Zedekiah (1)

Jeremiah 21:1–10; 37:1–21

As the Babylonians (or 'Chaldeans') advanced towards Jerusalem, King Jehoiakim died. He was briefly succeeded by his son Jehoiachin (or 'Jeconiah'/'Coniah'), who was taken into exile when the Babylonians first captured Jerusalem in 597BC. The Babylonians plundered Jerusalem but did not destroy it, and they replaced Jehoiachin with his uncle (Jehoiakim's younger brother) Zedekiah, whom they clearly expected to reign in deference and subservience to Babylon (2 Kings 24; Jeremiah 37:1–2). Zedekiah would do this only half-heartedly at best, and so he provoked Babylonian reprisals.

King Zedekiah clearly had a respect for Jeremiah that his brother had lacked. He felt that Jeremiah was the prophet to consult with regard to his and Jerusalem's future, and to do so with some hope of divine deliverance (21:1–2). But Jeremiah's response is unequivocal. Even if there might have been a time when repentance could have led to the LORD's delivering Judah from Babylon, that time is past. Now the only hope lies in submitting to Babylon and finding a future in and through, not apart from, Babylonian dominion over Judah and Jerusalem (vv. 3–10).

Zedekiah's other request to Jeremiah, 'Please pray for us', sounds straightforward and pious (37:3). But in the context of an army coming up from Egypt and a temporary Babylonian withdrawal, the subtext may have been, 'Will the Egyptians bring us freedom from the Babylonians?' (vv. 4–5). To this the answer is no, the divine purpose for Jerusalem and its inhabitants has not changed (vv. 6–10).

Jeremiah's message of submission to Babylon would naturally have sounded disloyal, even treasonous, to many people, so his simple action of trying to go from Jerusalem to his nearby home town of Anathoth simply evoked a hostile response, which led to his being beaten up and thrown into prison (vv. 11–16).

Zedekiah still wants to consult Jeremiah, presumably in the hope of hearing something different, something more hopeful-sounding, but nothing has changed (v. 17). Zedekiah also accedes, at least in part, to Jeremiah's request that he might not be left to die in his cell. But Zedekiah is clearly a weak king who cannot challenge his officials' suspicious and wrongful imprisoning of Jeremiah and set him free, but can only somewhat ameliorate the terms of imprisonment (vv. 18–21).

# 6  Jeremiah faces King Zedekiah (2)

Jeremiah 38

Even in captivity Jeremiah continues to deliver his message that the only hope for the future lies in surrender to Babylon. This message is heard by some of the royal officials as merely malicious, intending the people's harm rather than their good through undermining their will to resist (vv. 1–4), so they decide to get rid of Jeremiah once and for all, and Zedekiah weakly complies. However, they cleverly decide against trial and execution, which might make Zedekiah unhappy and in which public opinion might be unpredictable. Their purpose is to let the death be slow and unnoticed, leaving Jeremiah at the bottom of a muddy cistern to die of neglect and starvation (vv. 5–6).

For the first time, though, we hear of someone who cares about Jeremiah; strikingly, Ebed-melech is a non-Israelite and a slave, someone without the mindset of Jeremiah's fellow Israelites. Ebed-melech remonstrates with Zedekiah, who again complies, and Jeremiah is carefully rescued (vv. 7–13).

Zedekiah still wants to consult Jeremiah, although by now Jeremiah is weary of such consultations, as their only outcome is Zedekiah's inaction and danger to himself. Before Jeremiah says anything, then, Zedekiah has to swear that at least his life will not be endangered (vv.

14–16). Jeremiah's ensuing message, unsurprisingly, is unchanged: only in surrender to Babylon is there life and hope (vv. 17–18).

Zedekiah now speaks from the heart: he fears that he may be in no less danger even if he surrenders (v. 19). Jeremiah responds equally genuinely: trust and obey, and there will be life and hope (v. 20). Further, Jeremiah shares the content of a special vision of what will happen if Zedekiah will not surrender: as the women of his household are led into captivity, they will tell him that those he trusted have let him down and abandoned him (vv. 21–23). Just this once, he must trust Jeremiah.

Zedekiah's response is not that of someone who, for once, is going to act courageously. Rather, he urges Jeremiah to keep their conversation secret and, if pressed, to say that it was only about Jeremiah's own concerns for his safety; Jeremiah goes along with this (vv. 24–28).

Zedekiah tragically discovers the truth of Jeremiah's words and the cost of his weakness and cowardice, when his attempted resistance to the Babylonians ends in defeat, capture and pain for the rest of his life (39:1–7).

## Guidelines

Jeremiah speaks truth to power, but the powerful are unmoved: Jehoiakim is actively hostile, while Zedekiah havers indecisively. Jeremiah challenges the complacency of other prophets, but they are likewise unmoved: there is no mention of any of them changing their words or their ways. It is partly for this reason that there is a long tradition of seeing the life of Jeremiah as foreshadowing the way of the cross, a journey of darkness and opposition, where faithfulness to the LORD is supremely costly and where no fruit for one's labours is apparent. Can we identify comparable challenges for ourselves or others, and seek God's grace for strength to endure?

Read through a newspaper and note some issues that strike you as our challenges. Consider how we might appropriately intervene to deliver God's insights on these issues. Pray for those who are called to do this as part of their office, for instance, archbishops and bishops, or those leading aid agencies, concerned for the homeless or mentally ill.

Pray too for Christian politicians and other public figures who may want to obey God (as Zedekiah appears to have done) but are fearful of the consequences.

# 1 The cost of discipleship

**Jeremiah 15:10, 15–21**

Unusually within Hebrew prophecy, now we hear the voice of Jeremiah himself, speaking of how his prophetic vocation works out in his own life—what it means for him to be faithful to the LORD. It is not comfortable reading. (In today's reading I have passed over verses 11–14 as their sense is obscure. Insofar as these verses appear to represent words of the LORD, they are not part of what Jeremiah says on his own behalf.)

Somewhat like Job, though less forcefully, Jeremiah laments that he was ever born (v. 10a; compare Job 36), for who would want such a life? He does not bring the peace that everyone wants but, rather, is a focus of controversy and contention. Although particular resentment is often directed at people for financial reasons, because they either owe or are owed money, Jeremiah has had no such involvements and yet he is the focus of unremitting resentment (v. 10b).

He then directly addresses the LORD (v. 15a). He begins, like many a psalmist, by asking that God vindicate him against those who oppose him, because the insults aimed at him have come specifically because of his faithfulness ('on your account'). He wants to know that God is with him to help and uphold him, for he has been fighting for God. God's truth has brought him joy in his innermost being, and he has identified himself entirely with the LORD and his ways (v. 16). But finding joy in God has meant being unable to enjoy the company of his fellows in the usual way, for the enormity of Judah's alienation from God overwhelms and isolates him (v. 17). Why, though, does he say this? It is to reproach God, for in his unceasing pain Jeremiah feels let down. Far from being 'the fountain of living water' (2:13), the LORD appears to be a stream that looks plentiful but is in fact unreliable and runs dry (15:18).

The divine response is not exactly consoling. Jeremiah must remain faithful and the LORD will strengthen and deliver him, as initially promised (vv. 19–21; compare 1:8, 18–19). God never justifies himself, and the reality of his presence is not the same as our awareness of it.

# 2 A cry from the heart

Jeremiah 20:7–18

Life has become so terrible that Jeremiah complains sharply: the LORD has, in effect, lured him into a trap and beaten him up (v. 7a; some suggest that the imagery is of seduction and rape, but this is unlikely, as Jeremiah's imagination would have been less sexualised than ours). The reality of his ministry is that the only response he gets to his message about the LORD and the LORD's purposes (his own engagement with which brought deep joy to him, 15:16) is mockery, mockery and more mockery (vv. 7b–8). The expedient of easing the problem by trying to keep quiet is not an option, for that would deny the inmost reality of who he is (v. 9). Even those who once might have been his friends have turned against him and scheme to bring him down, so his isolation is complete (v. 10).

Yet his isolation is not complete because he knows, and clings on to, the assurances he has previously been given that the LORD is with him and will uphold and vindicate him against those who oppose him (vv. 11–12). Indeed, this leads to what looks like a sudden moment of relief and joy, a confidence that God has indeed delivered him in his hour of need (v. 13).

The moment of relief is only momentary, however, for (so the movement within the text suggests) Jeremiah now plunges into despair, which he articulates as intensely as does Job (vv. 14–17). The curse on his birth, and on the man who joyfully announced his birth rather than killing him there and then, is not just a cry of anguish, a wish that someone had aborted him; it is also, in effect, a further reproach to the LORD whose hand was upon him even before his birth (1:5). God has given him life and vocation, but it all adds up to no more than misery (v. 18).

Jeremiah, like the psalmist, does not speak about God (saying, for example, 'How could God allow this?') but rather *to* God. Even if no answer or resolution is forthcoming, this direct address, this determination to stay engaged with God, remains an all-important mark of faith. Moreover, we know that Jeremiah did not give in to self-pity or despair, but faithfully continued to speak for the LORD. It is not what one feels, but what one does, that counts. Jeremiah foreshadows Gethsemane.

# 3 A God-given hope

Jeremiah 29:1–14

After the first Babylonian capture of Jerusalem in 597BC, when King Jehoi-achin (Jeconiah) and others were deported into exile, Jeremiah maintained links with the exiles by letter (vv. 1–3). The content of this letter represents the other side of the now-familiar coin, that the only hope was to submit to Babylon and to find a future in and through, not apart from, exile in Baby-lon. A message that might have sounded unwelcome when people were still in Jerusalem may sound entirely different once they are in Babylon.

Their first priority is to think long-term about the exile (vv. 4–7), which is not about to end soon, despite the number of prophets who are clearly saying so (vv. 8–9; these prophets are akin to Hananiah, who claimed that the exile would end within two years, 28:1–4). The exiles must take seriously that Babylon is now their home for the foreseeable future, and they must therefore act as though they were at home, building houses, planting gardens, marrying and having children (vv. 5–6). Specifically, they must now identify with the people of Babylon in terms of seeking their welfare under God when they pray; for when Babylon prospers, its Judean residents will also prosper (v. 7). In a certain sense, Babylon is no longer 'them' but 'us'; the Judean exiles, while retaining their Judean identity, are now to be loyal citizens of Babylon. (Daniel and his friends exemplify the outlook and its possibilities: see Daniel 1.)

Babylon is not to be the Judeans' home for always, however, for a time limit is specified: 70 years (v. 10). This is an idiomatic way of saying that the exile will last a full lifetime (compare Psalm 90:10), which also means that any restoration will not be in the lifetime of those to whom Jeremiah is writing. An implicit reason for this long exile is now given: it is to provide time and opportunity for a fresh start, when a renewed sense of God's good purposes, in a place where they might have least expected them, should lead to a renewed turning to the Lord (vv. 11–12). In turn, this will mean that the people will be able to experience restoration as a gift of grace, a sign of renewed relationship (vv. 13–14). Since there will be no temple of the Lord in Babylon, their seeking of God will need to come not from any familiar patterns of religious life but rather from the heart.

# 4 Dare to act in hope

Jeremiah 32

Some years after writing his letter to the exiles in Babylon, Jeremiah is still in Jerusalem, where Zedekiah and others cannot bring themselves to heed his message of submission to Babylon with all that it implies. Rather, they imprison him (vv. 1–5; compare chs. 37—38).

Jeremiah, renowned for speaking of 'violence and destruction' (20:8) and, ironically, sceptical of Hananiah on the grounds that hoping for something does not make it so (28:5–9), now has to speak of hope and enact a sign of it, not just for the exiles in Babylon but also for those still in Judah. So it is perhaps unsurprising that the LORD gives Jeremiah a special reassurance that this is indeed from God, by predicting to him what will happen before it happens (vv. 6–8).

What is involved is simple—indeed, mundane. Jeremiah is to buy a field in his home town of Anathoth, just north of Jerusalem, and thereby fulfil a responsibility to keep it within his wider family, when for some reason his cousin Hanamel needs to sell it (compare the stipulation in Leviticus 25:25 and the practice in Ruth 3—4). But when a Babylonian army is besieging Jerusalem, and Jeremiah knows that the future will bring Babylonian victory and Judean exile, how on earth can a little piece of Judean real estate be of any significance whatever? Jeremiah sees that the meaning of this mundane action is immense (hence the great care to observe correct legal procedure, vv. 9–12), because it signifies a hope for the future and the restoration of regular life in a time ('a long time') after the current turmoil and mess (vv. 13–15). The field has no short-term future in Jeremiah's hands, but his buying it symbolises long-term hope.

Jeremiah himself is amazed that the LORD wants him to do this, and he turns to the LORD in prayer with words expressive of awed bewilderment (vv. 16–25). The LORD's response underlines the amazing nature of his merciful goodness, for Judah has done nothing but be faithless (vv. 26–35), and all that he will do to restore his people will show his divine initiative and power to transform (vv. 36–41). As he has plucked up, so he will plant (vv. 42–44; compare 1:10). Grace is amazing.

# 5  The basis for hope is God

Jeremiah 31:15–17, 31–37

In chapters 30 and 31, Jeremiah consistently speaks of hope for the future, a hope related to the letter-writing and field-buying we have already seen.

A first vision is of inconsolable anguish, of a mother who has lost her children and sobs unceasingly. The mother is Rachel, matriarch of Israel, and the children are Israel and/or Judah (v. 15) (an appropriate image also after Herod's massacre of young children around Bethlehem, Matthew 2:16–18). Yet the weeping can cease, and Rachel's work in bringing up her children will not be wasted, for the lost will be found, and those in exile will return home (vv. 16–17). This is not explained or justified; it is a gracious promise, to be received in trust.

The promise of a new covenant (v. 31) is famous, not least because of the way it is used in Hebrews 8:8–13. At first sight it looks straightforward: it describes a new relationship which, unlike the Sinai covenant, will be written on people's hearts so that communion between the LORD and Israel will be full and uninterrupted (vv. 32–34). But what does it really mean? The church may claim this new covenant, but it has to be admitted that its track record of faithfulness does not look to be an obvious improvement on that of Israel in the Old Testament, and teaching people to know the LORD is just as necessary now as it was in Jeremiah's time. It may be that the real point is the emphasis on God's gracious initiative (as in 32:37–41): there will be a new start, and this does not depend on Israel's becoming repentant but depends solely on God.

We saw in Jeremiah 18:1–12 that prophetic language is response-seeking, with an outcome contingent upon the response given. This is a general, but not invariable, truth. We have seen that disaster can be coming irrespective of whether or not there is repentance. So now restoration will come, irrespective of repentance or faithfulness. The point is that responsiveness matters, but the bottom line is the sovereign grace and faithfulness of God; hope is founded not in ourselves but in him.

The final assurance (vv. 35–37) underlines this thought. God's commitment to his people is unswerving, and their faithlessness does not nullify his faithfulness. Human faithfulness still matters, but the basis of hope is God.

# 6 A restrained hope

Where, and on what note, should we end our reading of Jeremiah? The book itself retells and expands on the terrible account of the overthrow of Jerusalem (ch. 52; compare 39:1–10); judgment and disaster are realities at which we must not blink.

For Jeremiah himself, things are hardly much better. The Babylonians spare Jeremiah's life (39:11–14), and there appears to be the possibility of a fresh start. He becomes part of a new community, no longer in Jerusalem but in nearby Mizpah. This community is led by Gedaliah, son of the faithful Ahikam, who accepted what Jeremiah said about Babylonian dominion and is a man of integrity. Initially things go well, but tragedy soon strikes. Gedaliah is assassinated by a man he refused to mistrust, and there is murder and havoc in the new community. Those who survive consult Jeremiah, who says it is God's will that they should remain in Judah under the Babylonians and that they absolutely should not flee to Egypt. But this is denounced as a lie, and the last we hear of Jeremiah is that these faithless people carry him off to Egypt, where there is no good prospect for them (Jeremiah 40—43). Jeremiah's story has no happy ending.

Yet interestingly the biographical narratives about Jeremiah end with a short narrative about his faithful scribe, Baruch, even though this narrative relates chronologically to the much earlier time when Jehoiakim burnt the scroll (45:1; compare ch. 36). Baruch's personal anguish has been similar to Jeremiah's (v. 3), and the LORD's initial words are hardly reassuring: disaster is coming for the whole of Judah (v. 4). Moreover, this is not a time for personal ambition, if Baruch might perhaps be tempted to anticipate future blessing and recognition because of his present enduring faithfulness. Disaster is coming on Jerusalem, and Baruch will not be exempted. Nonetheless, within the general disaster, the LORD does not lose sight of those he cares for, and Baruch receives a promise: his life will be preserved (v. 5).

The location of this episode suggests that we are to think of Jeremiah himself in these terms, as well as Baruch. Whatever the hope that Jeremiah has promised for others, for himself there is only hope reduced to its most basic form—staying alive, living rather than dying. 'He saved others; he cannot save himself' (Matthew 27:42): as Moses could only see but not enter the promised land, so Jeremiah bears witness to a hope that is more for others to enter into than for himself.

## Guidelines

Biblically rooted faith as a whole carries an astounding hope of life and joy for all eternity. Nonetheless, it can be salutary to remember that the reality of hope in this life may sometimes take the form of continuing just to keep putting one foot in front of the other, and not giving up. To put it differently, Jeremiah's life should surely encourage Christians to keep a steady focus on Gethsemane and Calvary, not rushing too quickly to the Easter tomb, even though it is there. A reading of Jeremiah should enable us to look more clearly at the tragedies and disasters of our world and to do so with a hope in God and his good purposes that does not falter (however one may feel). But this hope can never be glib.

'The reality of [God's] presence is not the same as our awareness of it.' How valid do you find this claim to be? How can we help one another to keep on believing in God's presence and care when life is challenging and tough?

Pray for any who you know are struggling at the moment.

Jeremiah sought to guide the Judeans in exile as to how best they might live. He implies a balance between regarding their present situation as a blip to be endured, or ignored as ultimately irrelevant, and settling so comfortably that they lose their commitment to God. Many suggest that the church in the west is 'in exile'. How might Jeremiah's insights be applied by ourselves?

Jeremiah buys a field from his cousin, even as the Babylonians invade, to symbolise long-term hope when others are in despair. What actions could our churches (locally and nationally) take to symbolise hope for other people?

# HOPE at harvest

Harvest brings Christian communities together to celebrate the provision of God. Traditionally, it signals that enough food has been gathered in for the coming year, although there may also need to be a recognition of difficult times in the year that is past. It is a time to reflect, to look back at the hard work involved in reaching harvest, and at the hand of God blessing that work with rain, fertile soil and enough sun to ripen crops. It is also a time to look forward with a sense of trust, believing that God will continue to provide.

Nowadays many of us are removed from the process of food production, but we can still take time to stop and thank God for his generous provision. Many people in our local communities may need us to lead the way, to help them thank God for all that they have or for getting them through tough economic circumstances. Churches running foodbanks in needy areas can help people to know that God has blessed them too with a share of the harvest. We might lead the celebrations this year with community parties, sharing some of all that we have been given with our neighbours and creating a community of thankfulness. To do this, though, we need first to be a thankful people ourselves.

22–28 September

## 1  First fruits

**Deuteronomy 26**

Giving back to God from what he has given us helps us to recognise our deep dependence on him. This is our focus at harvest time, when we remember where all our sustenance has come from. All that we have is God's, given to us as a gift, including life itself.

The Israelites gave the first produce from their land, not the leftovers or whatever could be spared. It was an offering of the best, dedicated to those who were in the service of God (the Levites, who had no land of their own and depended on gifts from others) and those in greatest need in the community (v. 11). What is your personal equivalent of the 'first fruits'? For many of us it will not be produce directly from the land, but there are other things that we produce, create or have a hand in; these are all given to us by God and of these we should give back to him generously. This can obviously apply to our money or time, but there will be other creative ways in which we could bring first fruits from our lives back to God. Another question to ask is, 'Who should the first fruits go to?' Harvest is a good time to re-evaluate our giving patterns and make sure that we are focusing our gifts on those in greatest need.

The main challenge in Deuteronomy 26 relates to ownership. What do I think is mine—mine by right, mine by hard work, or mine by my own initiative? This challenge is countercultural in many ways. For example, in our consumerist society, how can I live light to possessions? While others around are busy measuring their achievements, how can I live light to successful outcomes? With 'personal development' so highly valued, how can I live in the knowledge that even my very breath is a gift of a wonderful, gracious God?

Something of the secret to this way of living is in the prayer that the Israelites prayed each time they brought their gifts (vv. 5–10). This prayer reiterated all that God had done for them in their rescue from Egyptian oppression. They repeatedly told what the Lord had done for them; they recalled their reliance on him. As we offer our first fruits this harvest time, let's make sure we tell the story of God in our own lives and recall our total dependence on him, the giver of all things, who helps us to become thankful people.

## 2 God's hand in the harvest

**Psalm 65**

This psalm is filled with joy—joy in the abundance of God's blessing and provision, joy encompassing the created order as well as the people of God. The physical abundance flows out of spiritual abundance in the presence of God (v. 4). The people of God are, first and foremost, satisfied or filled by being with God, and this leads on to a celebration of the physical provision that we receive from God.

God has planned a created world with a rhythm that leads to harvest.

He has created a land that he cares for by watering and enriching it. This psalm points to a God who is actively participating in the nurture of our food, a God who is more closely involved than many of us in the UK with the production of the food we eat (v. 9). Many of us take no interest in the cycle of rains required to nurture the crops that produce the food that sustains us. This is a time to stop and thank God for being actively involved in the cycle of life that produces the food we rely on.

This psalm recognises that the hope of everyone, even to the ends of the earth, is in our God (v. 5). In some countries there is not enough food, the natural cycle is in peril from the impact of poverty or global warming, and people's lives are threatened. In other places, war has displaced people from their lands and there is great need. In a world where the population is set to keep climbing, food production is going to become more and more important. These global challenges may seem overwhelming, but there are ways in which we can get involved in praying, campaigning and working for the alleviation of poverty. There is so much food here in the UK, so much choice, and so little in some other countries, that this psalm encourages us to change our thoughts to action, so that we, the people of God, become the agents of God bringing hope to the ends of the earth.

# 3  When in need

Psalm 126

We have considered the need for thanksgiving to God for his provision of natural resources. But when there isn't enough food on the table or money in the bank, and no prospect of any improvement, what then? When we have barren fields emotionally or spiritually, with no experience of abundance, what can we learn from those who have faced real barren fields or famine? At this time of harvest celebration, what do we bring as an offering to God and what do we do with our sense of lack? How do we help others who are facing such hardships?

At such times, like the children of Israel, we can learn from the lessons of the past to help us face our present circumstances. Psalm 126 reminds us of Israel's experience of exile and return—that those who go out into barren times, weeping and carrying seeds to sow, return with songs of joy, carrying sheaves of wheat with them (vv. 5–6). When we are journeying through famine or desert times in our lives, we need the ability to remember the past and to recall the nature of the God who has led his people through past famine and desert, both literally and metaphorically.

We can remember, too, that God brings rhythms into our lives: as Ecclesiastes 3:1–8 tells us, there is 'a time for everything'. Periods of preparation, such as ploughing and sowing seeds, are difficult, but they bring a harvest. In our Christian communities at this time of harvest celebration, when we stand together in thankfulness, we should remember that some of us may still be living through a period of sowing in tears.

If you are sowing in tears, remember that it is in God's nature to bring a harvest for tears. He will not leave his people in a barren place but, by the rhythm that he has set, he will bring them through to harvest. This was true for Naomi, who changed her name to Mara, meaning 'bitter' (Ruth 1:20), after losing nearly everything she held dear. As God worked through Ruth, her faithful daughter-in-law, he changed Naomi's bitterness to blessing (4:14).

He is the same God who rescued his people Israel: he has not changed.

# 4  Extreme generosity

Luke 21:1–4

At harvest time, we make a show of giving. We carry produce into our churches and pile it up, but many of us are giving out of our wealth. God will notice those for whom bringing in a can of beans is a sacrifice because they are struggling in times of recession, just as he noticed the widow who gave her last penny to her God. No one else in the temple would have noticed her: they would not have run to speak to her or thank her for her generosity. She slipped in and her offering would have gone unmarked—except that Jesus, who knew the full story, highlighted her extreme generosity. As a result, it was recorded for all of us for all time.

As a volunteer worker in a hostel, one Christmas I was talking with a woman who asked, 'Will there be Christmas presents for us this year?' I said, 'Yes' and smiled, thinking how much she deserved a present, as she had so very little of her own. But she went on to say, 'This year I have had no benefits and the lady in the local café has kept me alive every day, giving me the leftover food at the end of the day. I wanted to know that I would get a Christmas present because then I can give it away to the lady in the café to say "thank you" as I have nothing else to give her.' I was moved by her example of extreme generosity.

How do we measure gifts? Who are the really generous people in our communities? Who are the generous people in our lives? Do we know who is practising extreme generosity around us? Do we measure who is generous by the world's standards, based on wealth and economic success, or, like Jesus, do we look to the heart of the giver? Let's not underestimate the small gifts of some in the community but, rather, celebrate them as much as we do the seemingly larger ones. If you are someone for whom a small gift in the world's eyes carries a big cost in your economy, be assured that Jesus still sees your extreme generosity and it will not be missed in the economy of eternity.

# 5  Outrageously thankful

Luke 17:11–19

Given that harvest is primarily a time to say 'thank you', I have realised while thinking about these readings how many of my own prayers are intercessory and how few are prayers of thanksgiving. Perhaps this time of harvest celebration could be an opportunity to focus on saying 'thank you' in demonstrable ways to God for all his gifts to us.

Luke tells us that there were ten lepers who cried out for help and asked for healing from Jesus. They did this together, making an equal effort in their intercessions, but only one returned to give thanks. How much easier we find it to cry out to God when we are in need of his help! This passage challenges us to recognise that we probably do not spend enough time dwelling on answers to prayer and expressing a thankful attitude.

Furthermore, in this passage it is a Samaritan—an outsider—who demonstrates thankfulness, and demonstrates it in an outrageous way. He is someone with all the wrong theology, born into the wrong people group, outside the acceptable people of God, yet he is the person who recognises Jesus as the healer and throws himself down in gratitude and worship before him. The other nine would have presented themselves to the priest and then followed the ritual sacrifices required by the law (Leviticus 14:1–32), saying 'thank you' in the appropriate way. As a Samaritan, the tenth man may well have been excluded from the sacrificial system in any case. Yet there is something about his almost improper thanks, with loud shouts and a physical demonstration of his elation (vv. 15–16), that is outside conformity but is exactly what the situation requires. If such a person ran into one of our churches, shouting loudly and throwing themselves on the floor in an expression of praise and joy, we can imagine someone trying simply to calm him down!

The Samaritan found a way to thank God—his own way—outside of his cultural traditions. Can we help people outside our churches to find ways of thanking God at harvest time that do not depend on our traditions and sacred spaces? For example, we might create a 'Thank God for the harvest' stand at a local farmers' market, where people can give some of their produce to help others and also write a thanksgiving prayer.

# 6 Learning to receive

Luke 10:38–42

Harvest is a time to say 'thank you' to God and a time to give, but might we also think of it as a time to receive from other people? As Christians we are often much better at giving than we are at receiving, at doing things for others than allowing them to do things for us. It can be disarming to be in a position where we are dependent on others for our needs. There is an exchange of power in giving and receiving that we can find uncomfortable.

Luke shows Martha as a great 'doer' who does not understand her sister's need to receive. Mary's actions in receiving from Jesus put her in a place of humility in relation to him, while Martha's service put her in the position of the one with something to give. In our society, having something to give means that we have a sense of power: we have the choice to grant provision or to deny it to others.

If we are the ones who always give and find it hard to receive, perhaps it would be good for us to stop giving, for a while. In my experience of mission, in the UK and Europe, one of the lessons I have learnt is to receive from those who have very little, and to allow less able people to do things, regardless of their ability. This empowers others; it helps them to give and enables them to serve, encouraging them to believe that they can make a valuable contribution. Asking for help makes us the weaker person in a situation, but it also allows another to feel a sense of worth in their ability to give to us or bless us.

In Luke 10:1–11, shortly before the account of Mary and Martha, Jesus sent out his disciples with nothing, making them entirely dependent on the people they met, the people among whom they were ministering, for everything that they would need. What an incredibly vulnerable place to be! Jesus himself came to our world as a baby, powerless even to feed himself, entirely dependent on his created parents. Perhaps there is a lesson to be learnt, this harvest time, about the value of being vulnerable and receiving from others.

## Guidelines

Here are some suggested prayers and actions for this time of harvest celebration.

- Pray for the welfare of our farming communities and all those in rural areas, who are relatively close to the means of food production.
- Work with our generous God in providing food for everyone, so that all will have enough to eat. Visit http://enoughfoodif.org, the website of the IF campaign that ran during 2013.
- Think about ways in which we could demonstrate, declare, shout, praise and fall at the feet of our God in thankfulness. How could your community of Christians get involved in an enormous 'thank you' as you gather for harvest celebations? What might that extravagant thankfulness look like in your everyday life in the coming week?
- When did you last ask for help? This harvest, are there people in your community whom you need to ask for help, to give them a sense of belonging and worth? Take a risk and ask!

# Exodus 1—20

Following on from Genesis, the book of 'beginnings', Exodus develops the plot of God's plan to save the world. Like many ancient stories, it begins with the birth of the hero—in this case, Moses—and generally follows his movements, but that doesn't mean the story is simply about the hero. Rather, the hero's life provides structure for the story. Along the way, we are introduced to some of the most important themes in the Bible—the call of God, God's deliverance of his people, his name among the nations, worship, and the ten commandments (law). The exodus is the watershed event of the Old Testament, as are the crucifixion and resurrection in the New, and contains much foreshadowing of the latter.

Scholars have shown that there were large non-native oppressed people groups in ancient Egypt. They have also noted that the law codes found in Exodus are very similar in structure to ancient Near Eastern law codes of the time. They have also found evidence of a people group very much like the Hebrews in Egypt, Sinai and the wilderness of Kadesh-Barnea. However, at present, we cannot 'prove' the exodus. This is because, outside of the two store cities, Pithom and Ra'amses, and Kadesh-Barnea, we cannot make a certain identification of any of the places mentioned. Furthermore, there is no sure connection made with particular Egyptian rulers.

Consequently, there have been generally two proposed datings of the exodus. The first is the traditional dating in the mid-15th century BC. This coincides generally with the biblical mention of there being 480 years between the exodus and King Solomon's temple (1 Kings 6:1), which we know to have been built between 1060 and 1020BC. A later date has been proposed, however, of the mid-13th century BC. This is largely due to archaeological evidence of a vast influx of people into the Judean hill country at that time. If this were the 'conquest' of Joshua, then the exodus would have been no more than 40 years earlier. Although this would seem to conflict with the distance between the exodus and the temple, many dates in the Bible are representative, perhaps indicating things other than strict chronology.

Quotations are taken from the New American Standard Version of the Bible.

# 1  A new Pharaoh

Exodus 1:1–21

As in the rest of the first five books of the Bible, the title in Hebrew is simply the first few words. Exodus literally begins, 'These are the names…' This connects us back to the story of the patriarchs in Genesis 46:8–27. Although much has changed—a new scenario with an increase from 70 persons to multitudes so great that even Pharaoh fears them—there is continuity. Exodus is still the story of God bringing about his initial creative purposes for humankind. First seen in Abraham, Isaac and Jacob, now it is traced through a community that becomes known as the nation of Israel.

At first glance, Pharaoh's plan to kill the male Hebrew babies seems confusing. Although it would reduce the military threat of Hebrew male slaves siding with his enemies, at the same time it would diminish his workforce. His plan may have been to keep the women for himself and his leaders (Hamilton, *Exodus*, p. 13). This idea is reinforced by his subsequent (probably deceptive) concession to Moses to let the men go and worship, leaving the women and children with Pharaoh (Exodus 10:10–11).

The midwives disobeyed Pharaoh, not simply because they found his command reprehensible but because they 'feared God' (v. 17). Somewhat curiously, their actions seem to go against God's own standards: they lied. However, telling the truth is not a straightforward command in the Old Testament. The ten commandments, for instance, only require a truthful witness in court (20:16). Telling the truth is viewed as part of a larger relationship that is based on truth. When such a relational framework doesn't exist, such as when people oppress others, there is no de facto obligation to tell the truth (Goldingay, *Exodus and Leviticus for Everyone*, p. 9). This explains other Old Testament examples, such as when God instructs Samuel to tell King Saul (who is seeking Samuel's life) that he is merely coming for a sacrifice to the Lord, when he is really anointing a new king (1 Samuel 16:2). Rahab and her family have their lives spared and are allowed to join the Israelites, essentially for lying to the king of Jericho concerning the whereabouts of Joshua's spies (Joshua 2:3–6). Hence, by lying, the midwives were not disobeying God, only their oppressor. In doing so, they showed that they feared God more than the threat of death that Pharaoh represented. According to Egyptologists, 'Pharaoh' means 'Great House'. Ironically, the midwives who defy the 'Great House' are rewarded with houses (families) of their own (Hamilton, *Exodus*, p. 15).

## 2  The birth of a deliverer

Exodus 1:22—2:25

Thwarted by the midwives, Pharaoh turns his cruelty upon the people (1:22): they are to throw their own newborn sons into the Nile. This gives rise to another recurring theme in Exodus—deliverance at the hands of women (see also 4:24–26). Not only are Moses' mother and sister involved, but even the daughter of Pharaoh himself gets drawn in to the plot. Moses' mother constructs something translated here as a 'basket' (v. 3), although it is the same word used in Genesis 6—9 for Noah's ark. Moreover, the language of verse 2, 'seeing that he was beautiful/good', parallels God's view of creation in Genesis 1. So, what the women do for Moses is like what God does for creation and for Noah, and, subsequently, what Moses will do for the Israelites.

As in the story of Queen Esther, there is no mention of God in this vignette. He appears to be working behind the scenes, through the courage, cleverness and compassion of the women. The life of his deliverer is in their hands. God doesn't so often work through the miraculous as through the character of people. What is shocking here is that his work even includes one who presumably does not know him—the princess.

Moses' name in Egyptian means 'son' (for example, TuthMosis means 'son of [the god] Tut'), but in Hebrew it sounds very close to a verb meaning 'to draw out' (v. 10). Pointing quite literally to the manner of his own rescue, it also foreshadows his mission. The 'drawn-out one' will himself draw the Hebrew slaves out of the water—the Red Sea.

Despite being reared in Pharaoh's house, Moses seems quite aware of his identity and even acts on the nascent impulse to defend the helpless that will eventually embody his calling—but he does so by killing an abusive Egyptian taskmaster (v. 12), reflecting the two-edged sword of God's giftings. The very thing that gives us a unique expression of God's heart can be our undoing. However, God does not seek to squelch Moses' personality, but to redeem it. Although Moses' decisiveness seemed impetuous and foolish at first, in Midian it appears rather heroic, as he rescues Zipporah and her sisters from abusive shepherds (Goldingay, p. 12).

# 3 The compassion of God

Exodus 2:23–25; 3:7–10

After following Moses to Midian, the camera pans back to the Hebrews in Egypt. Four different verbs are used for their sighs, cries and groans (2:23; 3:7). 'Crying out' is a special term reflecting the most anguished cry of desperation, typically of someone at the very end of their tether, with no other recourse or hope. It is used of Abel being ambushed by his brother (Genesis 4:10), of the victims of Sodom and Gomorrah (18:20–21), of the oppressed in Israel in the the time of the judges (Judges 6:6) and even of a woman giving birth (Isaiah 26:17).

These verbs are complemented by four terms for God's response: hear, remember, see and know (2:24–25). God 'sees', not by becoming visually aware but by taking a particular view of something—in this case, developing compassion for the Hebrews. Consequently, God's hearing and knowing refer to action. Just as I don't feel that my son has heard my instruction if he doesn't respond appropriately, God's 'hearing' is manifested in his intervention. He 'knows' in the sense that, in some way, he takes the experience of another upon himself and makes it his own (Fretheim, *Exodus*, p. 48). Finally, God does not 'remember' his covenant with Abraham, Isaac and Jacob as if he had forgotten it. To 'remember' something is to act in the light of it. The evils of slavery, though surely influencing his action, were not the deciding factor for his intervention. There were other people groups in Egypt who were similarly oppressed (12:38), but it is in the light of his covenant with the Hebrews and the purposes wrapped up in it that he acts. He acts to save *this* group from slavery because of his covenant with them. Their cry activates his covenantal response.

We could ask why God allowed all the years of suffering in Egypt before 'remembering' his people. If remembering means acting in the light of the covenant, then we see God doing just that. He had accounted for this time of slavery when he first made the promise (Genesis 15:13). The timing of God's intervention seems to have involved other contingencies, such as the need for the sin of the people whose land he would give to the Hebrews to have run its course.

# 4  The call and the name

Exodus 3:1–6, 13–22

Moses finds himself pasturing sheep on Mount Horeb (or Sinai). It is called 'God's mountain', but this is probably in hindsight: it is the mountain that later became known as God's. Otherwise, Moses would not have required warning about its holy status (v. 5).

The bush burned, but did not burn up. This alerted Moses that something supernatural was at work. Although the appearance is initially ascribed to the angel, or messenger, of the Lord (v. 2), God himself is subsequently said to speak from the bush (v. 4). This has led some commentators either to reduce the encounter to one with an angel acting on God's behalf, or to conflate the identity of the angel with God. However, the angel is not mentioned after the initial encounter. Also, only upon seeing that Moses has 'turned aside' does God begin to speak personally. It seems possible, then, that the angel was used to get Moses' attention and announce the Lord's presence (see Genesis 16:13; 31:13; Judges 13:22). When Moses turns aside to check it out, showing openness to the spiritual realm, the Lord intervenes. God often seems to allow something else to gain our attention—a coincidence, even perhaps an accident or illness—before giving fuller disclosure of himself.

God's own presence is required by the words that come next. God announces that he is the God of Moses' father, of Abraham, Isaac and Jacob. 'Father' in Hebrew can refer back many generations, so why not back to Noah or Adam? The selection of the patriarchs reflects God's covenantal connection. It is his promises to them—of descendants, land and blessing—upon which he now intends to act.

Similarly, if the Hebrews ask the name of the God who has sent him, Moses is instructed to tell them, 'I AM who I AM.' As their patriarchs knew God only as *El Shaddai* ('God Almighty', 6:3), any such request would probably not be for God's personal name, but information about him. Its shortened form is Yahweh, literally, 'He will be'. In the light of Moses' call, the character-reflecting nature of Hebrew names and Hebrew thought in general, this is not an abstract existential statement of 'being', but rather a statement of relationship. God is the one who will be with you, no matter where you go or what happens to you.

# 5 Resistance from unexpected quarters

Exodus 4:21–26

An odd episode occurs after Moses' call, in 4:24–26. After all the work that has gone into persuading Moses to return to Egypt, he is nearly killed by God himself. Again it is a woman—this time his Midianite wife, Zipporah—who saves his life, by circumcising their son Goshen, twice calling Moses a 'bridegroom of blood' (vv. 25–26).

The explanation for this strange episode comes just before it. The message that Moses is to deliver to Pharaoh is a threat. Since Israel is God's firstborn, if Pharaoh doesn't let the Hebrews go to serve God, he will kill Pharaoh's firstborn. Here in verse 23, 'to serve' refers to the 'servitude' to Pharaoh that the Hebrews are under, as well as being a primary verb for 'worship', which God desires. The Hebrews are to be released from one master in order to serve another. God's purpose is not simply to eradicate the evils of slavery but to enable and inspire and properly direct true worship.

However, this message to Pharaoh applies to the messenger as well. In verse 21, God commands Moses to do all of the *mophet*, or 'miracles', that God has put 'in his hand'. Literally, this applies to the miracle of turning the staff in his hand to a snake (4:3–4), but it refers also to the miracles of changing water into blood (4:9) and of making his hand leprous and clean again (4:6–7). However, *mophet* also means 'sign'. The paramount sign of the covenant between God and his people was circumcision. To be included among the people whom God sought to release in order to 'serve' him, Moses required the sign of the covenant. Otherwise, he retained his status as an Egyptian, like Pharaoh, outside the covenant and opposed to

God. It is likely that he *was* circumcised, as he was born into a Hebrew family. However, verse 24 is not clear about whether it was Moses the Lord tried to kill or Moses' own firstborn son. If the latter, then Moses indeed fell under the very threat that he was to deliver to Pharaoh. As a prophet, he needed not just to speak but to embody the message he brought.

# 6 A hardening

Exodus 6:28—7:6

Moses objects that he cannot persuade Pharaoh to let the Hebrews go because he is unskilled in speech (6:30). Yahweh's response is instructive: it is not Moses' job to make Pharaoh listen, just to relay what God gives him to say. His goal is not necessarily to persuade Pharaoh at all.

This is part of a larger plan to make Yahweh known, not only to Pharaoh but to the whole of Egypt (7:5). The plagues came in conjunction with Moses' proclamation, to demonstrate the powerlessness of the Egyptian gods. In fact, each of the ten plagues has been associated with a 'god' (or gods) of ancient Egypt. Thus, they undermined the pantheistic notion that divine beings were embodied in natural phenomena such as the Nile and the sun.

God's purpose was not only to make himself known but also to harden Pharaoh's heart in the process. This was so that he would have the chance to 'multiply' his wonders before the eyes of the Egyptians (7:3). The Hebrews themselves must also have been a target audience, as they had been exposed to the correlation between Egyptian religion and Egyptian political dominance for over 400 years.

The issue of divine sovereignty and human freewill is also raised, but the story is inconclusive on the matter. The occasions when God is said to harden Pharaoh's heart are equal to those when Pharaoh hardens himself. The order of these occasions is mixed, demonstrating that a hardening by God does not completely remove the ability of Pharaoh to harden himself at another time. Pharaoh also refuses to comply (7:14) before God performs any hardening, despite God's stated intent in 4:21. In fact, God knows of Pharaoh's pre-existing hardness of heart (3:19).

On the other hand, God is not helpless to act in the face of free will.

He can, and is repeatedly said to, 'harden' Pharaoh's heart, which must at least reflect some modicum of influence exerted over Pharaoh. However, this case is specific to Pharaoh, with the express purpose of glorifying God in the eyes of the Egyptians (v. 3). The most we can conclude from the exodus story is that God is free to override human will but does not make a habit of doing so. When he does, it seems to be merely a fixing of the course that the human has already determined, and is done for the greater good of humanity and the greater glory of God.

## Guidelines

Exodus expands the story of God's blessing in the world but also invites us into it. Initially, we are confronted with the midwives' fear of God. Theirs is a fear that creatively stands up to people who not only hold power over them but also oppress those over whom they have charge. In what ways do we take the risk of retribution upon our own heads in order to spare others, or simply to uphold God's honour?

We are then drawn in to Moses' call. Sometimes, despite trying to do the right thing, we find ourselves isolated. What perspectives or experiences do we possess that might put us in a unique position to address injustice or need—perhaps instances that we alone see?

The only sign received by Moses as a confirmation of his call came *after* he obeyed. He would worship God with the people back at Mount Horeb (Sinai). With what excuses do we answer the call of an all-powerful God, despite how 'legitimate' or 'realistic' those excuses might seem?

Why give an account of Moses' resistance to God? As all prophets are called by God, none is there strictly of his or her own accord. In today's world, leadership is quite often the result of self-promotion or popular election, but what kind of leaders would we have (or be) if they did not manipulate their way into position? What really motivates our decisions?

How often do we slink back from our calling because of our feelings of ineptitude or incompetence? Do we, like Moses, take upon ourselves the burden of success, and by so doing presume that we know the plans of God? Furthermore, do we, like Pharaoh, presume to be free to refuse him indefinitely? Although the reach of God's power, knowledge and grace is limitless, his patience is evidently not.

# 1 Yahweh's Passover

**Exodus 12:1–20**

Passover occurs in the month of Nisan (the latter part of March and the first part of April) and commemorates the spiritual founding of the Jewish nation. For the first time, they were no longer servants of another king, but a people under no one but God.

Although 'pass over' in the simple sense of 'miss out' or 'ignore' is commonly assumed to be the meaning of the verb *pasach* (v. 13), a better parallel can be found in Isaiah 31:4–5, where the Lord comes to wage war on the wicked at Mount Zion (who, incidentally, have also put their trust in Egypt). Verse 5 speaks of how he will hover like a bird over Jerusalem to protect it. So, in one fell swoop, he acts to destroy some while protecting others from that destruction. He is being selective about whom he punishes and whom he protects.

The selectivity of this plague is what demonstrates its miraculous nature. Firstly, the fact that only the firstborn were killed shows that it was not an epidemic or natural disaster, or even a genetic fault. It was an intentional act by a being who chose the firstborn to die, as a consequence of his firstborn being held in oppressive (and often deadly) slavery (see 12:40). Secondly, it was selective in terms of faith. Those who put this sign on their house showed their belief that God would kill the firstborn of their enemies, and their trust that he would protect the firstborn in their own house.

The comparison of Jesus to the Passover lamb, then, does not speak of atonement for sin, although other New Testament images do. The image is rather of God's grace and protection—a separation by his grace of a people for himself who put their faith in him as one who will protect them from punishment.

This passage contains the first mention of Egyptian gods (v. 12). Until this point, the conflict has been between Pharaoh (also seen as divine) and Yahweh. The gods mentioned here were at least supposed to protect their people. Thus, Yahweh's ability to march in at will and kill the firstborn of Egypt deals a decisive blow to their claim to power. This blow extends to Pharaoh himself, who was seen as the patron god of Egypt.

# 2 Song of victory

Exodus 15:1–21

Just as the exodus deliverance began with the women, so it ends with them leading in dance and song. The praise expressed here, as in many psalms, serves a double function. It gives God the thanks due for his saving of the people; at the same time, it is a witness to the peoples of the earth of God's great power, used on behalf of those who are in covenant with him (compare 9:16: 'in order to proclaim my name through all the earth'). Praise 'enhances the attractiveness of God' in causing his name or reputation to spread throughout the world (Fretheim, p. 164). The Philistines and other people groups do not tremble due to the word of some fugitive slaves, but because they have heard that this was the hand of Yahweh at work against a tyrannical oppressor. Let all who oppress others beware!

This song, some of the oldest writing in the Old Testament, contains elements of the ancient Near Eastern 'chaos' myth. In this myth, God conquers a chaos monster (often symbolised by a sea-serpent), creates the world, builds a sanctuary and is finally enthroned. Although the battle with Egypt was against a historical enemy, describing it in chaos myth imagery points to the fact that something more is going on. For example, although the Lord is pictured as a warrior, his weapons are not the swords and chariots of Pharaoh. He uses the wind and the sea, often seen as embodiments of 'chaos'. These are weapons appropriate to the cosmic foe that he is fighting. The mention of Egypt's gods (v. 11), the lack of any name for the Pharaoh, and the nature of God's weapons all point to a battle on a cosmic level. As Fretheim states, 'The Egyptians are also represented as [more than merely historical] in that *the chaotic forces of the world are concentrated there*' (Fretheim, p. 167). Hence, the battle is for God to re-establish creation order in the midst of Israel. He doesn't just rule over his people but over all creation, from within their midst.

# 3 Amalek

Exodus 17:8–16

Amalek was a descendant of Abraham (Genesis 36:12, 16), so, unlike the conflict with Egypt, this episode represents a 'family' affair. There is no reason given for the Amalekites' attack upon the Hebrews. They lived in south-eastern Canaan: perhaps they were threatened by Israel's march, or maybe they were greedy for Israel's flocks.

This is a divine battle, like the one with Egypt, but in this case the Israelites must fight as well. Joshua is mentioned here for the first time (v. 9), pictured as a military general who both selects his elite troops and leads the people to defeat the Amalekites. This is fitting, as his name means 'He saves'—essentially a different form of the name 'Jesus'. During the fighting, Moses must raise his staff for the battle to succeed. This demonstrates both God's power over the battle and, at the same time, Moses' need for help. Although he is the one through whom God speaks, who has had God's power surging through his staff, he too requires help. Aaron and Hur prop up his hands and help him access God's power.

The episode results in a permanent injunction against the Amalekites (v. 16). (Indeed, they will be fought with increasing success by Saul, David and Hezekiah, although they will still be around in the Persian period, in the form of the Agagite Haman, enemy of the Jews: Esther 3:1; 1 Samuel 15:8.) In fact, Yahweh himself makes a commitment to 'blot out' the name of Amalek (v. 15). Why should there be such a vicious response? It is not only for Amalek's vile treachery against the Hebrews: 'Because hands were lifted up against the throne of the Lord, the Lord will be at war against the Amalekites from generation to generation' (v. 16, NIV). Yahweh fights for his sovereignty not only to be recognised (as in the rescue from Egypt) but also to be established and defended. Affronts such as Amalek's bring about not only God's wrath but also his perpetual curse.

Whereas the initial victory over chaos was won by God alone, this subsequent battle has different implications. Firstly, it demonstrates that although the chaos enemy is defeated, it is not yet vanquished. There will still be occasion to fight until that becomes the case. Secondly, this time, divine power works in conjunction with that of humans (v. 12).

# 4 Jethro

Exodus 18:1–12

In stark contrast to Amalek stands Jethro, a Midianite priest. Like Amalek, he is related to the Israelites. The Midianites were descendants of Abraham through his third wife, Keturah (Genesis 25:1–2), and the fact that Jethro is Moses' father-in-law is emphasised twelve times in this chapter alone. Word of Moses' exploits has brought him to investigate, but, on hearing of the Lord's mighty deliverance of the Israelites, he doesn't tremble but rejoices (v. 9). Unlike Pharaoh, he now 'knows' that the Lord is above all gods (v. 11). Except, perhaps, for Hagar in Genesis 16:13 and the people who accompanied the Israelites out of Egypt (Exodus 12:38), Jethro is the first convert to the Yahwistic faith, and certainly the first whose conversion is described. Although the 'blessing formula' he utters can, in some instances, express only admiration, here it is a statement of faith, as it is in the context of worship (vv. 10–12). In a similar way to Naaman (2 Kings 5:15) and Nebuchadnezzar (Daniel 3:28), he is confessing Yahweh's superiority because of what he has seen.

Jethro takes care of his son-in-law by looking after his health. Just as Aaron and Hur came alongside Moses to bear one sort of fatigue, so Jethro supports him in a different sort. Jethro helps Moses to manage the people's 'inquiring' of God (v. 15). Inquiring of God through priests involved the divine dice, Urim and Thummim, and concerned decisions regarding warfare (1 Samuel 28:6, 15). Inquiries via prophets were on various topics, and are only sparsely mentioned in the whole of the Old Testament, but Moses faced these questions all day long. Although he quite clearly needed a change, Moses did have to display the humility he became known for, both in listening to a non-Israelite's advice and in relegating his duties to others. Here, however, God uses a voice from outside his own people to set Moses straight. His plan evidently worked, as we find later in the Old Testament that prophets are not inundated with inquiries, and no longer are those inquiries about legal issues. The primary reason for the latter is found in what God does next—giving the law.

# 5 Preparing for a divine encounter

Exodus 19

Although Sinai is often considered the place where the covenant was given, it is helpful to think of it as the place where the original covenant was developed (2:24; see Genesis 12:1–3). The first covenant only required Abraham to be circumcised and follow God's lead: the rest was God's responsibility. In Exodus, God shows that he has kept his part of the agreement by multiplying the people. He has made their name great, as other nations have heard of their deliverance and tremble (Exodus 15:14–16). Now, he is taking them to the land that he promised them.

No longer are the Israelites primarily passive recipients of God's covenant promises; they are to become Yahweh's treasure, holy, and a nation of priests (vv. 5–6). The combination is significant. Being holy, without being Yahweh's treasure, could deteriorate into legalism. Being his treasure, but not holy, could lead to licentiousness (Hamilton, p. 302). Being a nation of priests implies that their treasuredness and holiness are purposeful. As described in Isaiah 61:6, they will minister to other nations. However, a priest ministers first and foremost to God. This involves facilitating his presence in the world but also having special access to him.

This status and this mission require consecration. On this special occasion, the Israelites are to wash, abstain from sex and respect the borders of God's mountain (vv. 10, 12, 15). These acts reflect the value they place on hearing God's voice. Ritual cleanliness was a state that reflected separation from the 'unclean' or aspects of the world that represented a lack of God's order (such as death or disease). It also sought to reflect and focus on God as the creator of all life: therefore, things associated with human procreation were considered ritually (not morally) 'unclean'. Giving God his space reminded them of who he is—a God who must be met on his own terms.

Furthermore, preparation for meeting God shows an anticipation of his work. Verse 10 is one of four places in the Old Testament where 'to make holy' is used with 'tomorrow', and each instance looks toward a major move of God (see also Numbers 11:18; Joshua 3:5; 7:13). Hearing God's voice is a significant event: on this occasion, Moses is confirmed as God's prophet, and those witnessing it cannot deny God's presence.

# 6 The ten commandments

Exodus 20:1–17

The 'ten commandments' begin with a word about their author. God is the Hebrews' deliverer from Egyptian slavery, so what follows is to be understood not as a list of demands, but as their response to what God has already done for them.

The first command, or 'word' (v. 3), does not say that other gods don't exist, but that they are not to be honoured as gods. Only one holds that rank and power—Yahweh. Similarly, no images of God are to be made as aids to worship. Because no human portrayal can capture God's nature, idols cause us to worship a lesser god, more easily manipulated. Secondly, God already has an image—humankind. To make another is to default from our own role in imaging God to creation.

Taking God's name in vain (v. 7) is not simply swearing; it means to apply his name to anything he has not endorsed—whether a war, a building project or a church programme. Instead, we allow him to determine what is and is not of him.

Resting on the sabbath reflects God's own pattern of work and rest in creation. It reminds us of who created our world and continues to make it work. Rather than working that little bit harder to get ahead, or causing others to do so, we must trust that the time we spend honouring God will never be our undoing.

The last five commands centre on the family. As the commandments are generally directed at the heads of families, this means that honouring parents is not just for young children. It entails adults taking care of older parents who may be less productive or who interfere with their decisions (Goldingay, p. 81).

The Bible does not forbid killing *per se*—for example, in war, capital punishment or self-defence—but draws the line at premeditated murder. Stealing puts other families' livelihoods in danger, as does breaking the trust and intimacy of family bonds through adultery or lying about people in court. Wanting what others have means making their lives the judge of ours.

All of these commands essentially deal with trusting God to keep life right. By allowing the ten commandments to restrain our own solutions to life's problems, we show gratitude for the lives that God has delivered. He then takes his rightful place as our only saviour, free to express himself through his image and associations, and in the very bedrock of our lives.

## Guidelines

The battle in Egypt had cosmic implications. Sometimes, as in the books of Job and Daniel, there are cosmic conflicts going on behind apparently worldly matters. What battles are we fighting that may have more significance in the heavenly realms than we recognise? How do we measure the effect of our faith—in terms of merely human outcomes or of victory in the heavenly realms?

Although God must fight for us, and these fights often have heavenly counterparts, we too are called to fight at times. Are we waiting for God to fight all our battles for us or are we demonstrating our dependence upon his direction and power by putting our own necks on the line?

God chose a great leader in Moses, but even he needed to take advice. Often the pride that comes with being looked to by others for help keeps us locked into unhealthy patterns of service. We neglect ourselves and our families for the sake of ministering to others. Are we open to hearing God speak through a non-Christian or someone who is younger in the faith? Are we willing to release the very tasks that have, at times, filled us with a sense of importance?

Considering the preparation of the people to encounter God at Sinai, how do we separate ourselves from life to hear God's voice? How do we find the balance that comes from doing holy actions out of a sense of being treasured? How do we minister to God in seeking to bless him?

The ten 'words' (commandments) inform our response to God's love. What images of God have we erected that do him injustice? What have we prematurely ascribed to God or his will?

**FURTHER READING**

John I. Durham, *Exodus*, Word Books, 1987.

Terence E. Fretheim, *Exodus*, John Knox, 1991.

John Goldingay, *Exodus and Leviticus for Everyone*, SPCK, 2010.

Victor P. Hamilton, *Exodus: An exegetical commentary*, Baker Academic, 2011.

Alec Motyer, *The Message of Exodus*, IVP, 2005.

# The Bible and old age

This week and next we will be considering what the Bible has to say about old age. As with many topics, there is no single message: the Bible speaks with many voices, and we will encounter quite a lot of paradox and tension. If we think about it, this is not surprising, for the Christian Bible testifies to two covenants, which it describes as the 'Old' and the 'New'. The relationship between these two covenants is not simple: there is respect but also ambivalence and hostility. This is also true of relationships between the old and the young.

The mediators of the two covenants are quite different from each other. The patriarchs Abraham, Moses and David all lived to a great age and died of natural causes. They had many years to learn from their mistakes and develop wisdom, as well as the leisure to pass that wisdom on to their descendants. In stark contrast, Jesus of Nazareth, a single and childless man, died a violent death at a young age after an astonishingly short period of active ministry. The New Testament offers no clear and obvious model for growing old gracefully (although we shall see that there are several subtle hints). Why should it? The first Christians were expecting the end of the age and the imminent return of Christ. Issues of ageing were not their main concern.

We now know that we live 'between the times', and, with the extended life expectancy of our industrialised Western society, issues of how to live well at the end of our lives and how the young and the old are to relate to each other are more pressing for us. So we need to return to scripture, realising that our questions won't be answered directly, but assured that we will find divine principles and stories of God's dealings with human beings of all ages that will point us in the right direction.

Unless otherwise indicated, quotations are taken from the New Revised Standard Version of the Bible.

# 1 A vision of intergenerational bliss

Zechariah 8:1–8

The oracles of the prophet Zechariah date from the return of the people of Judah from their exile in Babylon to the holy city of Jerusalem. They are linked very specifically with the rebuilding of the temple (Ezra 5:1; 6:14) that took place around 520BC. Jerusalem had been laid waste by the troops of Nebuchadnezzar some 60 years earlier, and it appears that the whole area had suffered a period of social and economic breakdown. When the exiles who had yearned for their homeland finally returned, it would have been unrecognisable, and they faced the daunting, if not dispiriting, prospect of resettling and re-establishing a peaceful and prosperous society.

God speaks into this situation through his chosen prophet, and offers a vision of society characterised by a sense of *shalôm*—deep wellbeing due to his presence and favour. To use Jesus' term, it is a vision of the kingdom of God.

This vision is driven by God's burning and single-minded passion for his people. God is, as it were, desperate for them to be gathered together in safety and security. The community will be set aside as holy to God, who loves her as his bride (an idea that is taken up powerfully in Revelation 21:2). Like a husband, God will come to live with his people. His presence will be marked by the material fabric of the newly rebuilt and dedicated temple, but it will be marked more fundamentally by the social fabric of justice and peace that characterises the community.

It is, then, enlightening to reflect on the picture of the just and peaceful community that is presented here. It is one of gender balance and intergenerational bliss. Older people have a publicly visible and respected presence. They can move with dignity and security because each has a staff, which also acts as a sign of authority (as it does for bishops to this day). In this ideal community, old age has not been eliminated and the old are not marginalised. Moreover, alongside the old we find children playing. This is a community of joy, where there is time to play and where those who are not economically productive are valued. It is a prophetic challenge to our secular society, and also perhaps to our churches that so often segregate by age and sex and are seen to be failing if they attract 'only old women and little children'.

# 2 The rigours of advancing years

Psalm 71

Psalm 71 is a heartfelt cry to God from a man of advanced age. As he looks back over his long life, he recalls that God has been to him a trust-worthy 'rock of ages' throughout—a safe haven to whom he can run and hide in times of trouble. Yet this is not simply a relationship of protection. The psalmist is also full of praise and delight in the God he has known since his birth. There is joy and wonder.

Now, however, in the autumn of his life, the psalmist feels alone and vulnerable. We do not know the precise circumstances but, in the light of our knowledge of the physicality, psychology and sociology of ageing, we can make an educated guess. In ancient Israel it is likely that those few who lived to an advanced age were generally treated with honour. On the other hand, there were no pensions or welfare state to buffer the effects of their increasing frailty and dependency. In all societies, old age often brings with it illness, disability, poverty and bereavement. It can be a time of accumulated loss and deep loneliness. On top of that, the old are often stigmatised because they remind the young of their mortality: older people present them with an unwanted picture of their own futures. Attitudes to older people have always been ambivalent.

It is clear that the psalmist feels persecuted and stigmatised as 'God-forsaken' (v. 11). He has also seen many hardships and much misery in his long life. It's as if the difficulties he now faces seem too many; he feels too weary to run to his safe haven. He can only call out to his God.

As so often in the psalms, however, there is a turning point (v. 14). The psalmist draws on his life experience, the instruction laid down in his youth and practised as a spiritual discipline. He remembers that God is for him not only a safe haven but also a secure base, not just someone to whom he can run but someone whose love gives him the confidence to venture out into the world and live his life. We can almost see him standing up straight, as, by a tremendous act of will, he chooses to hope, leans on God and takes up one of the most important tasks of old age—passing on the true story of this same God to the next generation. Now he finds his sorrow mysteriously transformed to joy.

# 3  God will honour old age

Isaiah 46

Today we gain an insight into the mysterious transformation experienced by the psalmist in yesterday's reading. God speaks to his people through the oracles of 'second Isaiah' (Isaiah 40—55). This anonymous prophet was active just a little earlier than Zechariah, towards the end of the Babylonian exile but before the return to Jerusalem, and some scholars believe that this is one of the few female voices in the Bible.

The writer of Psalm 71 called out to his God, begging him not to forsake him in his hoariness (or grey hair, Psalm 71:18). Here in Isaiah, God answers using exactly the same Hebrew phrase, reassuring his people that he will save them 'even to hoar hairs' (v. 4, KJV).

The oracles of second Isaiah are distinctive in their strong emphasis on God's creative power, stressing throughout that God has been there from the beginning and is before and beyond all created things. God is not an object to be worshipped; he is instead the ultimate agent, the holy Other. To treat the Creator as a created object—even a 'spiritual' object—is idolatry. To help us see this, God repeatedly contrasts himself with the gods of the Babylonians (today's reading names Bel, the chief Babylonian god, and Nebo, an important figure in their pantheon). In doing this, God does not say 'I'm bigger and better than them!' He says something far more subtle, tender and moving.

God points out that just as the statues of these gods weigh heavily on poor beasts of burden, the gods themselves are nothing other than weighty human beliefs that have encumbered and misled those who hold them. God then says (and I paraphrase), 'For you it's the other way round: you don't hold me, I hold you. I don't weigh you down, I carry you. I have the power to do this because I uphold the universe. I have the right to do this because I have been around from the beginning; I knew you from your babyhood and all through the joys and hardships of your long life. Indeed I am your Creator. And because I am faithful I will carry you right to the end. I honour your old age.'

This imagery of God's taking his weary people in his arms and carrying them, as one might carry a little child, speaks powerfully of his love. It also speaks of his purposes that have been there from the beginning, for God is himself of old—the 'Ancient of days' (Daniel 7:9, 13, 22, KJV).

# 4 The tradition of the elders

Mark 7:1–13

Five hundred years have passed since the prophecy of second Isaiah. The people of God returned to their homeland and rebuilt their holy city but, since then, have been ruled almost continuously by a series of great imperial powers—Persian, Alexandrian, Seleucid and, finally, Roman. Meanwhile, with deep irony, the law by which they now live out their faith in the one who promised to carry them has, in the hands of some, become increasingly elaborate and burdensome. Elsewhere, Jesus makes this point forcefully: 'The scribes and the Pharisees sit on Moses' seat... They tie up heavy burdens, hard to bear, and lay them on the shoulders of others' (Matthew 23:2, 4).

In today's reading from Mark's Gospel, Jesus goes into this point in more detail. He has been accused of having no respect for the tradition of 'the elders'—the oral law that was passed on from rabbi to pupil. He appears to be a young man who cares nothing for the story of God that has been passed down from previous generations. Jesus responds by turning the accusation around, quoting from the oracles of the prophet known as Isaiah of Jerusalem (Isaiah 1—39). He quotes the first half of Isaiah 29:13, which continues, 'Their worship of me is a human commandment learned by rote.' Jesus is saying that the tradition of 'the elders' has become an idolatrous travesty of the divine law given by Moses.

In a brilliant move, Jesus then chooses as his example the treatment of older people by a tradition of 'the elders'. Their custom of prioritising goods and money as offerings to God has led to the neglect of dependent parents. The religious word *Corban* can be a cover for either misplaced piety or cynical lying that is utterly at odds with God's love for the aged and his command to honour parents (Deuteronomy 5:16).

There is a message here for many of us who may be money-rich and time-poor. Are we sometimes too busy with religious concerns and projects to give time to an older friend, relative or neighbour? We return here to the idea of leisured play in Zechariah 8:5: we need to cultivate the ideal society envisioned by God, where there is time just to be with and for each other. Jesus models this well. When he was at his busiest, so to speak, dying on the cross for the sins of the world, he took time to make sure that his mother would be cared for.

# 5  The foolishness of age

Job 32

In many cultures, older people are viewed as carriers of wisdom. They have seen much over the years and have had time to learn from mistakes and reflect on life. In contrast, the young are often viewed as impulsive, ignorant and foolish. However, research evidence challenges these stereotypes. It is true that the wisdom of wise people 'peaks' in their 60s and 70s. Nevertheless, many people live to a great age without ever attaining wisdom: 'There's no fool like an old fool.' More intriguingly, the time of greatest growth in wisdom is adolescence. Given their limited life experience, young people can be astonishingly wise.

In yesterday's reading we encountered a strange ambiguity and paradox. The tradition from ancient days that has been entrusted to our elders is vitally important, but elders sometimes betray this trust, creating a received wisdom that says more about them than about the original message. To put it another way, they tell their story, not God's story. It then becomes the task of the young to go back to the beginning and rediscover God's story anew. (See 1 Samuel 2—3 for a good example.)

Research from across the world has shown that the old often have difficulty in trusting the coming generation as 'keepers of the flame'. They expect the young to conform to their social standards and defer to their way of seeing things. In return, the young are frustrated by this lack of trust and the denigration of youth culture (Ephesians 6:4; 1 Timothy 4:12). In Britain today there is a feeling among the young that the Baby Boomer generation benefited from free education, full employment and an expansive property market, yet at the same time was blind to its selfish pollution of the environment, with no regard for its legacy to coming generations.

In today's reading we get a vivid sense of the intergenerational tension that can arise in determining fitness to impart wise counsel. The young man Elihu has had to sit through the speeches of Job's three older comforters. He is not impressed and he is bursting to speak himself. In the end, Elihu's speech, though eloquent, does not provide Job with the answer he needs but, with the wisdom of youth, Elihu shows one amazing flash of insight: life experience is all very well, but at the end of the day it is God's Spirit that imparts understanding to young and old alike (v. 8).

## 6  The unanticipated fruitfulness of age

**Genesis 15:1–6; 18:1–15; 21:1–7**

I recently enjoyed a visit with my family to a vineyard in Kent, which included a guided tour. The guide, who was very knowledgeable, explained to us that the highest-quality grapes come from vines that are advanced in years. These vines no longer produce the quantity of grapes that they did in midlife, but what they do produce makes the best wine. Our daughter rolled her eyes and said, 'That's going in one of Mum's sermons!'

It's true that this is an intriguing and charming natural image of the unexpected fruitfulness of maturity. However, our readings for today are far more radical, almost unnatural, for they tell the story of a couple who were not merely nearing their sell-by date but were way past it, and who nevertheless gave birth to a nation.

The whole concept is absurd—so absurd that when Sarah first hears of it she laughs, describing herself as literally 'worn out' (*balâ*). She is perhaps laughing at the absurdity of bearing a child after the menopause, but her immediate concern seems to be the idea of sexual pleasure—play and fun—between two clapped-out old souls. There follows a lovely pantomime 'Oh no I didn't! Oh yes you did' exchange between the

Lord and Sarah, where he seems to be playing with her. Finally, in due course, the Lord has the last laugh and Sarah bears a son—so of course he is named *Yishaq*, a pun on the word for 'laugh' (sahaq). Sarah's secret cynical laughter has become joyful public proclamation (21:6).

This story of Abraham and Sarah is foundational, telling as it does the story of the origin of the people of Israel, but it is also foundational in another way. The writers Richard and Judith Hays observe, 'The scriptures are filled with stories of God's breaking into the individual lives of older persons to confer a particular gift or vocation', with the result that 'older people can be unanticipatedly fruitful' (in Hauerwas et al., *Growing Old in Christ*, p. 11). It's into that human mix of wisdom and foolishness, faith and fear, cynicism and hope, so characteristic of old age, that God comes powerfully, transforming it into glory in his characteristically cross-shaped way.

The story of the aged Abraham and Sarah is foundational in that it sets this pattern for the strangeness and unexpectedness of God's actions throughout history: again and again, apparent 'no-hopers' turn out to be vessels of divine salvation.

## Guidelines

As we explore the range of attitudes to old age in the Hebrew Bible, it becomes clear that 'older people' are primarily *people*. God honours them and deals with them with tenderness and care. He sees them as capable of bearing fruit right up until the end of their earthly lives. On the other hand, they are neither idealised nor above criticism. Sometimes they need to be taught a lesson by the young, who, with all their strengths and weaknesses, are also primarily *people* and, as such, honoured by God.

*With a propitious eye, and a great pity, behold the miseries of mankind; put a speedy period to all our sins and to all our calamities: hear the sighings of the distressed, the groans of the sick, the prayers of the oppressed, the desires of the poor and needy; support the weakness of them that languish and faint; ease the pains of them that are in affliction, and call to thee for help. Take from the miserable all tediousness of spirit and despair: pardon all the penitents, reform the vicious, confirm the holy, and let them be holy still; pity the folly of young men, their little reason and great passion; succour the infirmities and temptations of the aged, preserving them that they may not sin towards the end of their lives; for Jesus Christ's sake.*

Jeremy Taylor (1613–67), an Office or Order for the Administration of the Holy Sacrament of the Lord's Supper

# 1 New wine

**John 2:1–11**

The account of the wedding at Cana is placed very firmly at the threshold of Jesus' public ministry in John's Gospel. This is a story that is all about time. The changing of water into wine is '*the first* of his signs', which not only reveals Jesus' true identity but also marks the passing of the old age and the dawn of the new. The occasion is a wedding feast, an image often used by Jesus to signify the *eschaton* (Matthew 9:15; 25:1–13). The *eschaton* is usually understood to refer to the 'last things'. It may, however, be more helpful to think of it as the threshold(s) between two orders of being that are utterly and unimaginably different from each other: heaven breaks through to earth (John 1:51); the kingly rule of God draws near to the lives of human beings (Mark 1:15); the old age gives way to the new (Luke 16:16). These thresholds are essentially clashes of culture, points of contact marked by stress, strain and pain as much as by joy—rather like childbirth (John 16:21; Romans 8:22).

We see this in the tense exchange between Jesus and his mother in today's reading. Jesus uses a Semitic phrase (v. 4) that directly opposes him to Mary (who is of the previous generation). The issue is one of timing. Mary hasn't actually asked Jesus to do anything; she has merely expressed her recognition that he has the power to help in this embarrassing situation. Jesus sees even this as premature. Nevertheless he takes action, doing something apparently strange that only makes full sense when we recognise this occasion as a threshold: he turns his attention to some water jars. These are the sorts of vessels used for the purification rituals that were the basis of the controversy in our reading from Mark 7 last week: they symbolise the 'tradition of the elders'—the *ancien régime*.

The fact that Jesus chooses to use these vessels indicates his desire to engage with the tradition of the elders. The fact that the vessels are filled to the brim with water that is then transformed into wine of the highest quality indicates that the original intention behind this tradition has been both generously fulfilled and superseded in him: the good wine has been kept until *now* (v. 10).

The Ancient of Days is doing a new thing. The older generation, then, faces a dilemma: should it cling to the old ways or embrace the new?

## 2 Betrayed by the elders

**Matthew 16:21; 21:15–23; 26:3–4**

In the history of the church, plagued as it has been by anti-Semitism, there was for many years a deeply unfortunate understanding of Jesus as the universal man, perhaps even the blond Aryan man, betrayed to his death by the Jews. What has been less often observed, but is closer to the facts, is that Jesus was a young man betrayed to his death by an older generation—the elders. The precise chronological age of the elders doesn't really matter: they were respected senior members of their community.

The attitude of these seniors is set against the words of little children in Matthew 21:16. Here Jesus again uses paradox, quoting a very *ancient* scripture (Psalm 8:2) to make the point that the very *young* may be given insights that can overturn the wisdom of their 'elders and betters'. The next day, Jesus encounters a fig tree that, unlike the elderly vines of the Kent vineyard I mentioned last week, is producing no fruit at all. As with the 'elders', we don't know the age of this tree. The point is that, like them, it is not bearing fruit and thus cannot offer any hospitality to Jesus. This is quite different from the attitude of the ageing Abraham, who offered lavish hospitality to God's messengers and was thus able to receive their apparently absurd message. Crucially this was because, even though Abraham was undoubtedly a flawed human being, he had faith in God (Genesis 15:6). Notice how Jesus goes on to stress the importance of faith (vv. 21–22) and to link it with receiving from God.

Having returned to the temple to continue his teaching, Jesus' authority is then challenged by the elders. Jesus doesn't have a recognised priestly heritage. Indeed, his father is unknown. He has burst on to the scene from a disreputable northern village (John 1:46) of no historical significance. He travels from place to place with 'nowhere to lay his head' (Matthew 8:20), avoiding putting down the roots that might establish him as a known and trusted quantity in any one community. And he dares to teach his grandmother to suck eggs.

The priests and elders seem obsessed with judging Jesus of Nazareth in terms of his past. For them, history—patrilineage or lifetime experience and achievements—determines authenticity. This makes them blind to all that is self-evident to the children, who simply respond to what they see before them here and now: this young man bears a kingship conferred from of old.

## 3  Your old men shall dream dreams

Luke 2:25–38

The priests and elders in yesterday's readings were backward-looking and reactionary. Their eyes were closed (either intentionally or subconsciously) to the true identity of Jesus. What a contrast to Simeon, who is described as 'looking forward' (v. 25) and says of himself that 'my eyes have seen' (v. 30)!

Simeon is usually assumed to have been an older man (quite reasonably, given that he seems to have been waiting a long time and to be in the final period of his life). Less reasonably, he is sometimes also said to be blind. Luke actually mentions neither of these things. Instead he concentrates on Simeon's righteousness, piety and openness to the Holy Spirit (recall Job 32:8).

Mary and Joseph have come to the temple in conformity with the ancient tradition for the priest to make atonement for Mary's postpartum ritual uncleanness (Leviticus 12:8). The irony is that she carries in her arms a newborn who will make atonement for the whole world (1 John 2:2); he is the glory of Israel and the revelation to the Gentiles. Simeon sees all this. His vision is of the *shalom* in Zechariah 8 extended to include all nations.

The wedding at Cana marks the threshold between the old and the new in John's Gospel. This encounter with Simeon in the temple marks an equivalent threshold in Luke's Gospel. In Luke's second volume (Acts) we are reminded that in the 'last days' the Holy Spirit will be poured out on all, 'and your sons and your daughters shall prophesy, and your young men shall see visions, and your old men shall dream dreams' (Acts 2:17, quoting Joel 2:28). Here we have an assurance that at the end of the age, while the powerful representatives and vested interests of the old order may reject Jesus, many older people will welcome him with joy. These are spiritual people, not living exclusively in the past but alert to the present and with a vision for the future.

There is another sign of the dawning of the new age—gender balance (recall Zechariah 8:4–5). So here we find Anna, who is unquestionably old. Anna has had a long and full life. There must have been many memories of the good (or bad) old days that she could have shared with passers-by, but she doesn't: this very old woman can't stop taking about a very young baby she has just met. She looks to the future and becomes the first Christian prophet.

# 4  As good as dead

Hebrews 11:8–16

In today's reading we return to Abraham, the archetypal model for faith in God. The letter to the Hebrews was written to encourage and inspire a community of Christians who seem to have become tired, jaded and disheartened. The aim is to restore hope by reminding them both of the supremacy of Jesus and of his ability to empathise with human weakness. Along the way, several inspirational figures from Israel's history are also brought into play, and Abraham is the most important of these.

Earlier this week we considered Abraham's hospitality to God. Here we are reminded that Abraham was also prepared to risk all because he trusted God. He was, like Simeon and Anna, forward-looking. Abraham was prepared to endure an earthly lifestyle marked by provisionality because he knew that this was only a small part of God's great purpose for him and his people. He lived on the edge and his eyes were turned heavenwards.

Hebrews uses the pejorative phrase 'as good as dead' (v. 12) to describe Abraham (as does Paul in Romans 4:19). It's a rhetorical device. The writer is essentially saying, 'Look at this old man: he was utterly past it but he was caught up in God's vision. He didn't look back with nostalgia or regret; he didn't cling to what he had; he strained forward to inhabit the heavenly places, and he bore unimaginable fruit! If a geriatric like him could do it, you lot have no excuse!'

The fact that Abraham was at his most generative in very old age is perhaps not so absurd after all. It tells us something of the special spiritual gifts of this time of life, for very old people are standing on an edge, poised at a threshold—an *eschaton*. They are living in the end times of their own lifespans (as are the terminally ill young). This can be a very rich time for looking back and drawing the threads of life together to make a good ending, but it is also a time for preparing to cross the threshold. To use a Celtic phrase, it is a 'thin place'.

Put another way, it's as if some old people have reached a mountain-top and can see new vistas, as yet hidden over the horizon from the rest of us. This gives a whole new meaning to the phrase 'over the hill'. If we only take the trouble to attend to them, perhaps these mountain-top visionaries will tell us what they see.

# 5  When you are old

John 21:15–19

All through this series of Bible readings we have been presented with a series of paradoxes. Older people have the privilege of passing on God's story, yet they often need the young to help them discover it afresh. Older people can have great wisdom and great foolishness; God can transform both for his marvellous purposes. Jesus was highly critical of the 'tradition of the elders', yet he respected the spirit of the Torah that required children to honour and care for their elderly parents. The older generation betrayed Jesus, but some older people had a special prophetic insight into his identity and mission.

Now comes the deepest paradox: the young man Jesus of Nazareth is both the eternal *logos* who existed before Abraham and also the future promise that Abraham saw and greeted from afar. Jesus claims as much in John 8: his opponents chide him for being 'not yet fifty' and he responds with the immortal words, 'Before Abraham was, I am' (John 8:56–59).

This final paradox sets out both Jesus' youth and his great age. In today's wonderful reading from the end of John's Gospel, Jesus shows his insight into the restrictions of old age alluded to by the psalmist in our reading last week. In old age we give up our autonomy. Our liberty may be restricted by regulations that prevent us from driving or making our own decisions. Our agency may be diminished by physical infirmity or cognitive impairment. We do less and less for ourselves and more and more is done for us and to us. We may well be stigmatised.

John tells us that when Jesus describes the loss of autonomy that Peter will undergo as an old man (v. 18) he is referring to Peter's death— traditionally thought to have been by crucifixion. This is something that Jesus knows all about at first hand. Now we see that although he died young, the nature of Jesus' passion and death was an intense version of the ageing process. In his book *The Stature of Waiting*, W. Vanstone draws attention to the fact that the 'passion' of Jesus is the 'passivity' of Jesus in which he becomes an object, handed from pillar to post, about whom decisions are made and to whom things are done—stigmatised, weakened and enfeebled. He undergoes the rigours of advancing years.

Out of this experience Jesus has some words for Peter and for us all about growing old gracefully. They are simply these: 'Follow me.'

# 6 Intergenerational church

Mark 15:21; Romans 16:13

For our final reading in this series, I have chosen two very brief and apparently obscure texts, both of which mention a character called Rufus. We can't be sure that they talking about the same person, but many scholars have concluded that they are. When Mark (whose Gospel is thought to have been written in Rome) introduces Simon of Cyrene, he adds the detail that he is the father of Rufus. This would be unnecessary unless Rufus was a well-known figure among the Christian community in Rome: 'You know Rufus? His dad actually carried the cross.'

Some years earlier, Paul has sent greetings to Rufus in a letter to this same community, and also mentions Rufus' mum, describing her literally as 'his mother also of me'.

Paul's asides are often intriguing but also tantalising, as they hint at so much but give so little concrete information. What did he mean? In other letters Paul uses maternal imagery to describe his own ministry of establishing and growing Christian congregations, talking of breastfeeding (1 Corinthians 3:2), being in labour (Galatians 4:19) and gently tending (1 Thessalonians 2:7). So perhaps he meant that this woman acted as a kind of spiritual director or mentor to him.

We shouldn't be too quick to spiritualise this phrase, however. Paul was, after all, a flesh-and-blood human being with physical and psychological as well as spiritual needs. He was, by all accounts, of unprepossessing appearance (2 Corinthians 10:10), lacked confidence in public speaking (1 Corinthians 2:3–5), and was argumentative (Acts 15:39; Galatians 2:9) and generally difficult to be with. He struggled with some sort of chronic affliction (2 Corinthians 12:7), most probably visual impairment (Galatians 4:15). On balance, it seems likely that Paul was unmarried. He was always an outsider—not one of the Twelve, and 'untimely born' (1 Corinthians 15:8). Paul knew the love of Christ but he also must have craved human mother-love, and there is a strong suggestion that he got it from the mother of his friend.

In Romans 16:1–6 we are given a tiny glimpse of an early Christian community living at the dawn of the new age. It was both gender-balanced (notice how Prisca and Aquila head the list of names in verse 3) and intergenerational, marked by the tender loving care of an older woman for a younger man. The wonderful vision of Zechariah 8 was already being realised.

## Guidelines

A loving community in which all are valued reflects the created order. The degree to which a community values people of all ages and ethnicities and both sexes, recognising and encouraging the gifts of all, dispensing tender loving care to all as needed and making space for joyful celebration *together*, is a measure of its conformity to the kingdom of God. This is true of communities that call themselves 'church' and of society at large. Older people have a special part to play in these communities as those who remember and hold the gospel story for future generations, as visionaries whose loosening ties to this earth may give them a heavenly perspective on the present, or simply as generous founts of love. They are an underappreciated treasure.

*Praise the Lord! Praise the Lord from the heavens;*
*praise him in the heights!*
*Praise him, all his angels; praise him, all his host!*
*Praise him, sun and moon; praise him, all you shining stars!*
*Praise him, you highest heavens, and you waters above the heavens! …*
*Mountains and all hills, fruit trees and all cedars!*
*Wild animals and all cattle, creeping things and flying birds!*
*Kings of the earth and all peoples, princes and all rulers of the earth!*
*Young men and women alike, old and young together!*
*Let them praise the name of the Lord, for his name alone is exalted;*
*his glory is above earth and heaven.*
*He has raised up a horn for his people, praise for all his faithful,*
*for the people of Israel who are close to him. Praise the Lord!*
PSALM 148:1–4, 9–14

---

**FURTHER READING**

S. Hauerwas, C.B. Stoneking, K. Meador and D. Cloutier, *Growing Old in Christ*, Eerdmans, 2003.

A. Morisy, *Borrowing from the Future: A faith-based approach to intergenerational equity*, Continuum, 2011.

W. Vanstone, *The Stature of Waiting*, DLT, 2004.

U. Staudinger and M. Pasiopathi, 'Correlates of wisdom related performance in adolescence and adulthood' in *Journal of Research on Adolescence*, Vol. 13, 2003, pp. 239–268.

For more details on Anna, see J. Collicutt, *Jesus and the Gospel Women*, SPCK, 2009, pp. 62ff.

# Matthew 11—14

Those who have read notes on Matthew 1—13, in previous issues of *Guidelines*, will already be acquainted with many of the leading themes of Matthew's Gospel. Jesus has been introduced to us on a variety of levels. We have learnt how his extraordinary birth signalled the arrival of an exceptional human being. We have discovered how Matthew proclaimed loudly and clearly from the beginning that Jesus was the Messiah and, by contrast, how Jesus himself was reticent. In Matthew 9:30, having healed two blind men, he 'sternly ordered them' not to tell anyone. Of course, they completely ignored him. They had called upon him as the 'Son of David', a messianic title, but Jesus told them to be quiet.

Here we encounter what is sometimes called 'the messianic secret'. Jesus rarely claimed the title of Messiah, most probably because, before his followers could use it properly, he needed to redefine its meaning and what people understood by it. His works of healing and deliverance were all part of this redefinition. There was a wide range of expectations of the 'Messiah', and Jesus was not a messiah in the sense of a national and political leader who would make a bid for power in order to liberate the land. Perhaps this is what Judas (10:4) was expecting and why he became disillusioned.

No, Jesus was a healer, full of the power of God, who mediated transformation and hope to people. He preached repentance and the kingdom and gathered a community of followers who were learning to do likewise. In the verses that follow, we read more of this new way of understanding Jesus and the salvation he brought to Jews and Gentiles alike. We cannot set an agenda and make him into whatever we would like him to be. Salvation does not lie in that direction. We have to let him be who he is, and the fullness of his identity will not be clear until the whole gospel has run its course.

Quotations are taken from the New Revised Standard Version of the Bible.

# 1 John the Baptist

Matthew 11:1–15

We have met John the Baptist already as the one who baptised Jesus and whose mission was closely related to Jesus' own. Despite the assurance with which John pointed to Jesus (recorded in John 1:29), it appears here that even John harboured doubts about him. Matthew, following what we have already gathered, affirms Jesus as the Messiah in verse 2, but John seeks reassurance. By this time, John has been imprisoned (near the Dead Sea, according to Josephus, the historian), but he sends word by his disciples, asking Jesus, 'Are you the one who is to come?'

Why such hesitation? It seems that Jesus does not match even John's expectations, whatever they were. Jesus does not send back a straight reply and, once more, does not identify himself as the Messiah. This may have been because, had John's jailers overheard such a claim, he too might have been arrested. Jesus' reply points John instead to the mighty works he has been doing. From these it could be gathered what kind of Messiah he was.

John may have entertained doubts about Jesus but Jesus was absolutely sure about John. His message to him ends with a benediction. John should see Jesus for what he is and not as a stumbling-block. Jesus himself saw John as the great prophet and messenger who, according to Malachi 3:1, was to precede the Lord's own coming to his temple. This, of course, says as much about Jesus as it does about John. John was Elijah (Malachi 4:5), preparing the people for the 'great and terrible day of the Lord'. Jesus was the Lord in question and this was his day. For this reason, John could be described as the greatest person ever to have arisen, not because of his personal qualities but because of the position he occupied at the end of the age of expectation and the dawn of a new age. The least in the kingdom of God would be greater than he because the new age was the time of fulfilment of all the hopes of Israel. The kingdom may have suffered opposition from the violent, but the law and the prophets were about to be fulfilled in the person and work of Jesus.

# 2 The terrible day of the Lord

Matthew 11:16–24

We are tempted not quite to believe that the 'great and terrible day' of Malachi 4:5 is really going to be all that terrible. If so, then the words of this section should be a warning to us. The coming of Jesus is surely a great day. Who could doubt this when we are witnesses to his healings and exorcisms and have seen the tender mercy that he has displayed to so many? These are not acts of terror—far from it. Yet we have already detected a very different undertone. The demons that Jesus cast out were terrified of him (8:29). His own disciples were at times overawed by him (8:27). Jesus has already issued fearsome warnings to fellow Jews who fail to welcome him (8:12). In the present verses, Jesus rails against the Galilean towns that have not received his preaching or attended to the mighty works he has done.

The fact is that the people are fickle. They are like children in the marketplace who do not know what they want and cannot make their minds up. In short, they are playing games, as is often the case when it comes to matters of religion. People are impressed by signs and wonders but treat them as entertainment. They enjoy a religious argument but do not speak from deep conviction. In spiritual things they are as insensitive as swine (7:6). It is the triviality and lack of seriousness that riles Jesus to anger and leads him to warn the cities that he knew so well of the danger of their condition.

The heart of the matter here is that he is the one by which they will be judged. Their response to Jesus is the criterion by which judgement will be meted out. To reject or ignore him is a dangerous thing to do, whether it be active or passive. Sloth in our approach to God is as deadly as outright rejection of God. Failure to feel this, and to feel it deeply, is a symptom of our disease. Without a certain sense of terror in the presence of a holy God, we demonstrate that the God we prefer is a domesticated one who is unable to disturb our complacency.

# 3 The mediator

Apathy towards God is not the only theme of this chapter. The words we study in these verses are among the most significant in all the Gospels. To begin with, we have a very rare glimpse of the inner life of Jesus. The first three Gospels in particular major in his words and deeds. They move at a fast pace, almost a whirlwind, as we encounter the active Jesus ministering to his generation. They say little about his emotions or his self-consciousness, so when we do gain a glimpse of them it is all the more enticing.

Here we see Jesus praying to the Father. He combines a sense of the greatness of God as Lord of heaven and earth with an equal sense of God's closeness, as *Abba*, Father. This is what the Sonship of Jesus means in intimate, relational terms. If the Lord's Prayer is somewhat lacking in the element of thanksgiving, such is not the case here. Jesus thanks the Father for the fact that divine and holy things have been revealed to the disciples. For this reason Christ has come into the world to do the Father's will, and his work is not in vain. But even more, in these words we see expressed what we have seen embodied in previous chapters: Jesus is the Mediator. He has a unique relationship with the Father and the Father with him. The two know each other exhaustively. On verses such as this we ground the Christian belief that 'Son of God' is not simply a messianic title. It embraces an exclusive relationship between Father and Son that reaches back into eternity. Yet this relationship is no longer exclusive, because the Son is free to reveal the Father to others and to draw them into the same intimacy, whereby they too may know the Lord of heaven and earth as *Abba*, Father.

If there is a central claim that the Christian faith has and that it can share, this is it. God waits to be known as Father. Through the Son alone, this communion may be known and entered into by those who look to the Son and trust him to draw them into the divine life. Jesus' words, inviting us and all to come to him, make perfect sense in this perspective.

# 4 Lord of the sabbath

Rabbinic law (not the Old Testament itself but rabbinic interpretations of it—in this case, of Exodus 34:21) forbade 39 types of work on the sabbath, of which one was 'reaping'. A strict interpretation of the law meant that to pluck ears of corn on the day of rest was a violation. Only a minority of Jews might insist on this interpretation but Jesus comes into conflict with them here.

The law made provision for the poor and foreigners by insisting that the corners of the cornfields should be left unreaped, so it was quite in order for the disciples to do what they did. Jesus cites an example from the Old Testament of a time when overriding human need superseded the letter of the law: David (a prestigious figure, loved by God) ate the ritual bread in the house of God (1 Samuel 21:1–6). In addition, the priests would regularly violate the day of rest by working in the temple. This incident gives Jesus the opportunity to advance a more humane understanding of the law. Mercy towards others trumps the letter of the law. The sabbath was given not to be a burden but to be a humane ordinance ensuring that both humans and animals were allowed to rest.

The use of the title 'Son of Man' (v. 8) could imply either that Jesus, as the Son of Man, had authority to interpret the law in the way he did, or that the welfare of human beings should be preferred when a law was not working for their benefit. This gives latitude in interpreting the law with human well-being as the final criterion. Most Jewish teachers of Jesus' day would have accepted this without difficulty.

Embedded in this incident is a most important saying: 'I tell you, something greater than the temple is here' (v. 6). For Jewish believers, there was nothing greater on earth than the temple in Jerusalem. It was the house of God, the dwelling place of the Almighty, the site of atonement and forgiveness. It was the place to which Israel ascended in order to receive blessings from the priests. Yet Jesus claims to be greater than it. The implication that Jesus would replace the temple was one of the claims that brought about his final execution.

# 5  Further conflict

Again, Jewish law decreed that it was only lawful to heal on the sabbath if a person's life was at risk. If an illness were chronic but not at crisis point, or merely temporary, then the problem could wait until the next day. It was a matter of contention whether an animal's suffering might be alleviated on the sabbath. Jesus indicates here what most agreed, that a sheep would be rescued from a pit, especially if it were the owner's only one.

By now it is obvious to us that Jesus' inclination is always to heal. Entering a synagogue, he finds a man with a withered hand. The man does not ask to be healed, and such a condition could have waited till the next day, but Jesus' opponents are watching him, looking for an excuse to find fault with him. Jesus is well able to debate with them and, once more, shows a degree of humanity that is typical of the law, even if not always of its interpreters. It should not escape us that Jesus does not, in fact, do any work here. He simply asks the man to stretch out his hand and it is restored. The passive case is used, indicating that Jesus did not actively bring healing, not even by touching the man. It was simply granted by God.

Jesus wins the argument and, at the same time, is not even guilty of the fault of which he is being accused. His opponents are struggling to make any charges against him stick, so they are moving to the point where a conspiracy to destroy him is developing. With these dark hints we begin to move slowly towards the second half of the Gospel, which will see the tide turn against Jesus and propel him towards his death. The years of popularity are not to last for ever.

# 6  The Servant of the Lord

Jesus is still about the task of redefining what it means to be the Messiah. For this reason we encounter once more 'the messianic secret'. Although Jesus openly heals, he instructs those whom he does heal not to make him known (v. 16). The redefinition is not complete.

From where, on a human level, did Jesus derive his own ideas about what it meant to be the Messiah? As we examine his own teaching we may conclude that two Old Testament books were particularly influential upon him—the books of Deuteronomy and Isaiah. The central part of the prophecy of Isaiah, which is a prolonged reflection on the catastrophic suffering of exile and captivity in Babylon, introduces us in a series of 'songs' to a mysterious Servant of the Lord. Matthew cites one of the songs in this section (vv. 18–21; see Isaiah 42:1–3), speaking of a chosen servant of God on whom God's Spirit rested and who would bring forth justice. He identifies this figure with Jesus. The longest and most profound song is found in Isaiah 53 and speaks of a suffering servant whose vicarious death will be the means of redemption. Christians cannot read these verses without thinking of Jesus, who fulfils it at every point.

These are the words that Jesus would have read, which would have informed his understanding about his own vocation and about the kind of Messiah whom God would send. This was revolutionary thinking, and people could not yet understand it. The crowds that implored him for healing were prepared to own him as a messiah according to their own understanding. Many of the Pharisees could see Jesus only as a deceiver operating in the power of Beelzebul (one of many names for the ruler of demons). Jesus argues with them that, if demons cast out demons, then the demonic kingdom is hopelessly confused and so divided against itself that it is unable to stand. To the contrary, Jesus is casting out demons by the power of the Spirit, and this is the sign that the kingdom of God, which overcomes the kingdom of darkness, has arrived. Jesus is its agent. He is the one who will bind the strong man, Beelzebul himself, and plunder his goods—the human lives that have been held in thrall to him. Of this, all his mighty and compassionate works are a sign.

## Guidelines

What does Jesus mean by blasphemy against the Holy Spirit and the unforgivable sin (Matthew 12:31–32)? People are sometimes persuaded that they have committed this sin and are without hope. Yet the fact that they are troubled in this way indicates precisely that they have not committed it. Only the rejection of forgiveness is unforgivable. When people identify the work of the Spirit as that of Beelzebul, or the devil, it is evident that they have lost all spiritual tenderness and are unable to receive what the Holy Spirit is offering them. If they persist in this attitude, they are indeed unforgivable, because the Spirit is the one who brings forgiveness. Forgiveness is a relational category before it is a judicial one and it cannot flow to us without our reception of it. So blasphemy against the Spirit is not a one-off happening but a continuing hardening of the heart against God and the one he has sent, Jesus Christ.

Those who oppose Jesus in the passages we have read demonstrate that hard-hearted attitude, but this is not to say that they may not at some point repent and receive the benefits that the Messiah brings. The challenge to ourselves is to read these narratives with receptive and trusting hearts. Then they will influence and shape us for the good and we will bear fruit for God.

# 1 Looking for signs

Matthew 12:33–42

Jesus has performed many signs and wonders up to this point. He has authenticated his ministry with healings and exorcisms in abundance. He has also pointed to those signs as illustrations of his messianic mission. When some scribes and Pharisees ask him for further signs, it is difficult to know what they want that they have not already seen. Jesus is not impressed by this request. It is not made by those who are in personal need of healing or deliverance so it cannot be described as a plea for help. We can only conclude that the hearts of those who are asking are not sincere. They come into the 'evil' category already identified by Jesus: out of the abundance of their hearts they speak, but their hearts are filled with bad things, not good (vv. 34–35). The request for a sign is made out of unbelief, not receptivity mingled with trust.

Signs are given, not obtained by aggressive demand. In the latter case, Jesus knows very well that even the most dramatic sign would not be welcomed with faith. It would probably be explained away or attributed to Beelzebul. Requests like this are, in effect, demands for God to prove himself to us on terms that we can accept—but if we lay down the terms, this means we are 'putting God to the test' in an arrogant way.

There is just one sign that is given for all to ponder and which is itself the authentication of Jesus as Messiah—the resurrection. Jesus refers in verse 40 to the three days Jonah spent in the belly of the big fish and sees it as an illustration of what will happen to him before his resurrection. The fact that the Jews counted any part of a day as a whole day makes this allusion easier for us to grasp: Friday, Saturday and Sunday are counted as three whole days because Jesus spent all or part of each of them in the tomb. This is the great sign that is given and is to be believed. It marks Jesus out as greater even than Solomon at the height of his reign (v. 42). His resurrection by God's power should be enough for all.

# 2  The family of Jesus

Matthew 12:43–50

At first reading it is not easy to see how this story fits the context. It describes what needs to happen when an evil spirit departs from someone. The vacuum needs to be filled or the latter condition will be worse than the former. We know that, as an exorcist and healer, Jesus had practical experience and wisdom in this area, and this story demonstrates his wisdom. Its real purpose here is probably to emphasise the impossibility of neutrality. After an evil spirit leaves, the person needs to be filled with something else, not left empty. Something wholesome and definite needs to come in. If the space is empty, then it will be filled by more and worse spirits than in the first place.

Jesus has been travelling around Galilee and Judea casting out evil spirits, liberating space, but of itself that is not enough. If the liberated space should not be left empty and neutral but should be filled, what better to fill it with than the kingdom of God as proclaimed by Jesus? Neutrality and agnosticism are not enough. The decision to welcome and follow the Christ is all-important. Many of Jesus' hearers were wavering at this point.

This sets the context for the appearance of Jesus' mother, sisters and brothers. It is generally assumed that, by this time, Joseph has passed away. After Jesus' resurrection, his relatives played important parts in the nascent church, James and Jude (or Judas), for instance, becoming leaders of the church in Jerusalem. Before the resurrection, however, they are sceptical of Jesus' claims, being bound to him by kinship but not by discipleship. When they appear on the scene and wish to see Jesus as he is speaking to the crowds, Jesus overrides their request because his loyalty to the bonds of faith that tie him to his disciples is greater even than his loyalty to his birth family. True kinship exists among those who do the will of the Father. The spiritual ties of the messianic community are deeper and stronger even than the biological ones of family loyalty. The natural family is not absolute but is subordinate to the higher demands of the people of God.

# 3 The sower

Matthew 13:1–9

We can imagine that the house mentioned here (v. 1) is the one in which Jesus lived in Capernaum. The town is close to a natural amphitheatre, which works well when somebody speaks from a boat offshore. We are now reading a section of the Gospel in which the writer strings numerous parables together, like pearls in a necklace. Jesus' use of stories and parables is outstanding. It is difficult to think of any other religious teacher whose words were so effective and memorable when presented in this form.

In his daily work as a carpenter (see 13:55: the word is *tektonos*, from which we derive 'technician', and suggests that the range of skills and practical know-how of Joseph and Jesus after him was wider than in carpentry alone), Jesus would not have been confined to a workshop but would have travelled to where the work was. He would have had ample opportunity therefore to observe the work, customs and conditions of his fellow Galileans. We should imagine that Jesus was highly observant and aware of the things happening around him. All of this he puts to good use in his parables. The first he tells is interpreted later in the chapter, so here we will confine ourselves to a few aspects of what we read.

The sower in this story should be understood as Jesus himself in his work of preaching repentance and the kingdom of God throughout the cities and countryside around him. The seed is the message of the kingdom, which has penetrated people's hearts and is germinating in them. The sower scatters seed widely and indiscriminately on the ground in the hope that, given time, it will bear fruit. All of this is clearly reminiscent of what Jesus was doing and the way he understood himself.

The parable ends with the invitation for anyone with ears to listen (v. 9). Of course, we all have ears so there are different levels of hearing involved here. There is superficial listening and listening in depth, and it is to the latter that Jesus calls attention. All may hear superficially but not all may hear in depth what is being said. To hear in depth requires a spiritual disposition to connect with the story in depth. We need this if we are to engage with it.

# 4 The place of parables

Matthew 13:10–17

The use of parables is so characteristic of Jesus that his disciples seek an explanation of why he adopts this method. His response is surprising. We naturally assume that Jesus uses parables to make his message plain for ordinary people. We imagine that they are like illustrations of the kingdom, designed to illuminate. But in fact Jesus uses them to make the truth obscure, to intrigue and puzzle and to do so in such a way that only those who have the right disposition will grasp what he really wishes to say. He distinguishes between the disciples and others. To the former, the secrets of the kingdom have been given and, because they already have receptivity and openness, more will be given to them. But those who have none of this will end up with nothing.

Jesus quotes the ironic words of Isaiah 6:9–10 about those who will listen but never understand. Isaiah attributes the people's lack of response to the state of their hearts: their hearts are dull and so they are hard of hearing. The preconditions for true hearing are not present when hearts are disposed to apathy or self-preoccupation. Something mysterious has to happen in the depths of the heart to enable Jesus' hearers to welcome and receive the truth that the parables contain.

The disciples are blessed because the appropriate disposition has been given to them. Their eyes now see what many before them have longed to see: the time has now come and their hearts have adopted the right disposition of repentance and receptive faith to enable them to appreciate the truth that the parables contain.

It may also be the case that the meaning of the parables is not immediately obvious even to the disciples. They have to question Jesus about what he means because it takes time to enter into a parable: the story needs to be reflected on and absorbed before we see its full significance. Our minds need to be transformed before we get the point. Parables have to be lived with over time so that their full impact can be appreciated. They are like slow-release medicines that yield their benefits gradually. Wrestling with the parables is a complex but rewarding activity when our hearts are right.

## 5  Interpreting the sower

Matthew 13:18–23

As it happens, it is easier to assign meaning to the parable of the sower than to many of the others. It includes elements of allegory, and, to assist the disciples in their understanding, Jesus adds an explanation. We have already understood that Jesus is referring to his own messianic mission. The different soils on to which the seed is sown represent different responses to him and his message. Some hearts, like the path, are hardened and closed. Some people, like the rocky ground, show an immediate joyful enthusiasm but quickly lose it. Some make an apparently genuine response but other concerns, anxieties and problems overwhelm the response and all is lost. Finally, though, there are those who receive the word with understanding and produce fruit out of all proportion to the seed originally sown. They persevere to the end. These are those, minority though they may be, who make the mission abundantly worthwhile, and they are represented by the very disciples Jesus is instructing (although we should never forget Judas).

All of these responses were encountered by Jesus and, it must be said, his experience has been that of the Church through all its generations. Any active witness or evangelist could tell exactly the same story as Jesus when it comes to 'profit and loss'. There is acute disappointment, of course, in those who do not receive the word or persevere in it. At the same time there is comfort in the fact that even Jesus experienced the same, and so we are not above our Master in this regard or any other. The emphasis of the parable is on the fruitfulness of those who respond fully and so outweigh the disappointments. There is also encouragement in the suggestion that, as we spread the word, there will be those who do respond. The Church's task is to find them. Sowing the seed will produce a harvest. The proclamation of the word will not be universally triumphant but it will have an impact on some, and they will be fruitful in God's service.

# 6 Parables of the kingdom

**Matthew 13:24–32**

Jesus offers here two parables. By this time we are becoming attuned to his methods and, with the right disposition, can gather their meaning for ourselves (although Jesus adds an explanation later in the chapter). The parable of the wheat and weeds is a reflection on the mixed nature of the messianic community. Although people are taken at face value as disciples of Jesus, there may be those in the church who are insincere. They are like weeds sown by an enemy in the night and intermingled with the genuine seed. In the company around Jesus there was one such person, who has already been mentioned, namely Judas (10:4). Should such people be rooted out so that the church can be pure? The problem is knowing who they are and how to deal with them.

In this parable Jesus suggests that to try aggressively to root out the insincere would risk doing harm to those who are sincere. We can imagine that it would turn the church's attention inward and create a climate of suspicion. The church will never attain perfection this side of the last judgement. Better to live with the imperfect situation and allow God, in that final judgement, to do the sorting. Obvious troublemakers might, of course, be excluded (18:17), but even they would then become subjects to be evangelised. Even Judas is an example of divine providence because, although he betrayed Jesus, he did (paradoxically) play a part in handing Jesus over for arrest and trial, and thus in the work of redemption.

The second parable here also contains a paradox. Proverbially, the mustard seed was regarded as the smallest seed, but the person who plants it is amazed when it grows into the largest of trees (mustard trees grew normally to the height of a bush). So with the kingdom: although, at its beginning in Jesus' ministry, it might appear small and insignificant, in time it will grow to an immense size and provide security and shelter for many. We who are alive now are able to witness to the truth of these words, and the fullness of the kingdom is still to come.

## Guidelines

Jesus was one who provoked others to a decision. Matthew's Gospel portrays the fact that he was not universally welcomed. The response of many of his fellow Israelites confirms John's verdict that 'he came to what was his own, and his own people did not accept him' (John 1:11). We have argued that although Jesus did not come intentionally to divide, this was a consequence of his coming; in the wisdom of God, it was known beforehand that this would be so. Even Jesus' own family appear not to have believed in him at this point in the Gospel, preparing us for the fact that his resurrection from the dead would be the major turning point for them also (1 Corinthians 15:7).

It is a sad fact that the truth does divide, because humans prefer to oppose it. They are happy with their illusions and delusions. Although we claim to be rational and to judge on the basis of evidence, actually the great majority of us look for arguments and evidence that will suit our own preferred and predecided beliefs. 'Reason' is, much of the time, simply 'rationalisation' rather than honest thinking. Of course, this is as true for Christians as it is for anybody else. When we study the teaching and life of Jesus, we should, if we are lovers of the truth, open ourselves time and again to encounter him in the pages of scripture so that we avoid having a Jesus whom we can manipulate to serve our own images or preferences.

Jesus confronts us with searching questions. What is most difficult for many people is not the ethical teaching that Jesus gives, or the things that he does, but the claims that he makes for himself. Yet this is the heart of what it means to be a Christian. Of course, we do believe in ethical principles about the good life, but, most of all, to be a Christian means acknowledging the testimony that Jesus bore to himself, confirmed by his mighty acts and vindicated by the resurrection. Jesus is the Messiah, Son of Man and Son of God. He has a unique and distinct relationship with the Father that he mediates to those who trust him. He was endowed with the Spirit to be the one who fills the highest expectations of humankind, whether Jew or Gentile. There is no getting beyond this. We either believe it or we do not, and in this lies his greatest challenge.

# 1 More parables of the kingdom

### Matthew 13:33–50

It is reiterated here that when it came to communicating with the crowds, parables were Jesus' medium of choice. In private, with his disciples, he would then unpack what the parables meant. He does that here with the parable of the wheat and weeds.

Of the other short parables recounted in this section, two have to do with the great value of being within the kingdom of God (vv. 44–45). To 'possess' the kingdom is so much to be desired and so inherently valuable that to surrender all for its sake is both reasonable and joyful. It is a good business deal. The kingdom provides the motive for radical and risky action. Other things pale in importance besides it.

The kingdom of God represents the future. It is like yeast that gradually permeates through the dough. In time, the kingdom will expand and its power will be manifest. It is also like a fishing net, cast abroad and bringing in a catch: in the end, there will be a reckoning, like non-kosher fish being separated from the kosher, and there will be a reward.

The kingdom fizzes with divine energy. For Jesus it is the main thing, more important than anything else happening in the world, even though the kingdom is not 'of this world' but is a gift from the God who is beyond it yet closely engaged with it. Given the remarkable expansion of the Church, the community of the kingdom, since Jesus' day, we must deem his words to be in the process of progressive fulfilment. The kingdom is both now and not yet. Its power is already being experienced in the lives of Jesus' followers and has already had great impact upon the world, but it is not yet complete. Its full power has yet to be experienced; its final coming is still awaited, but it is still like treasure in a field or like a fine pearl of great value. It is still worth living for.

# 2  A prophet with honour

Matthew 13:51–58

Matthew has Jesus rounding off the collection of his parables with a summary statement that gives us a clue as to how he regards himself. Scribes (the scholars who wrote and interpreted the Hebrew scriptures) generally get a negative mention in Matthew, but here they are described positively, as is the scribal task: a good scribe brings teaching from the Hebrew scriptures but also has new ways of looking at it and applying it (v. 52). This was Jesus' own method and he commends it to his disciples. He lived in full consciousness of those scriptures and the story they told, but also had new insights and interpretations to offer as to how the story should continue. In this he was also acting as a prophet (v. 57), interpreting and applying the word of God for his day.

Jesus' experiences in his home town of Nazareth prompted him to see himself in the tradition of prophets who were often disregarded by their contemporaries. Astounded by the works that he did and at a loss to explain from where they all came, his compatriots took offence at him. As we read this account, we learn some valuable details: there is no mention of Jesus' father by name but he is identified as the local carpenter whose trade Jesus would have followed; Mary is mentioned as his mother by name; Jesus had at least four brothers who are named and a number of sisters. These details contribute to our knowledge of the composition of the church in Galilee and Jerusalem after the resurrection. But the people with whom Jesus had grown up found it hard to accept that someone with whom they were so familiar could be emerging as one so significant. Familiarity, as they say, really does breed contempt. As a consequence, the power of Jesus to do mighty works was reduced.

Here again we learn something about faith. In contrast to unbelief, which closes down all options, faith is receptivity mingled with trust. Where this environment is present, the power of Christ is at its most free; where it is reduced, his power is curtailed. Churches that manifest receptivity mingled with trust are most likely to see Christ's power at work.

# 3 The death of John the Baptist

Matthew 14:1–12

The basic events of this section are confirmed by Josephus, the Jewish historian. Jesus has been closely connected with John from the beginning, his own ministry being portrayed as arising from John's. To fulfil a prophetic role was always a precarious business, since part of the task is to confront the powerful with inconvenient facts. John had been put in prison by Herod Antipas, son of Herod the Great, because of open criticisms he had made. Herod was slow to execute him because, in the eyes of the people, he was a prophet, but in a series of events that must be held as typical of the degenerate class that Herod represented, John was at last executed, his head being dished up for Herodias.

John was a martyr, but he had made a large impression on his contemporaries. Despite his having pointed to Jesus as the Messiah, some of his disciples remained attached to John (in fact, John the Baptist still has followers—the Mandaeans of Iraq). There is a contrast to be seen here between the disciples of John, who retrieved his body and buried it, and the disciples of Jesus, most of whom fled in fear of their lives when he was arrested. At least, this gives evidence that the disciples of revered prophets like John cared about their burials. Later on, it was some of Jesus' female disciples, with the help of Joseph of Arimathea, who would perform the same duty for Jesus in place of those who had fled.

Jesus was not just abandoned to the common grave, however, and this is an important fact for attestation to his resurrection. His burial place would need to be known to confirm that he had risen. Herod entertained the view of Jesus that he was John the Baptist raised from the dead and attributed his great powers to this fact (v. 1). This appears also to have been a widespread view among the people (16:14). John the Baptist now being dead, however, with his mission fulfilled, the burden of proclaiming the kingdom falls on Jesus' shoulders and hints of his forthcoming passion begin to emerge.

# 4 Feeding the crowds

Matthew 14:13–21

The link between this passage and the former one might suggest that Jesus sought a lonely place to reflect on the death of John and what it might mean for himself. Whatever the reason for his retreat, however, his fame and popularity are such that the crowds hunt him down. Jesus' own compassion for them will not allow him to ignore their needs, and his healing ministry goes on all day, to the point where the people need food.

We now encounter the only miracle to be reported in all four of the Gospels. (In 15:32–39, Matthew also describes a second feeding miracle, this one, in all probability, among Gentiles.) The fact of its being repeated in all the Gospels suggests that it possessed particular meaning for the Gospel writers. We are, of course, at a loss to explain how so little food could become enough to supply the needs of 5000 men plus women and children, with twelve baskets of leftovers. The miracle is much more than one of mutual sharing. Because of its context in a deserted place, the event is a clear reference to the miraculous feeding of Israel with manna in the wilderness (Exodus 16). Jesus is the one who, like God, provides abundantly for Israel and feeds them with heavenly food. In John 6:35–40, Jesus will identify himself, after this event, as the living bread that came down from heaven.

Practical lessons drawn from this miracle indicate that, however little we have, if we bring it to God and if it is hallowed and blessed as the fish and loaves were by Jesus, then our efforts and their benefits to others can be multiplied beyond calculation. The whole incident, set in the context of Jesus healing the multitudes, is one of profound generosity. The crowds are fed to the point of being filled, and still there are a full twelve baskets left—the number of the tribes of Israel. The God revealed in Jesus is a God of overwhelming generosity and kindness towards all of Israel and to all nations. This is welcome good news, is confirmed by all that we know of Christ's compassionate ministry, and is the motivating factor behind the mission of Christ.

# 5 Jesus on the water

Matthew 14:22–27

The disciples leave the scene by boat and Jesus resumes the purpose for which he came to this deserted spot in the first place. After he has managed to disperse the crowds, he goes up the mountain by himself to pray. Mountains are often associated in the Bible with closeness to the presence of God. We should not just take it for granted that prayer was an essential part of Jesus' spiritual discipline. The work of praying for the sick would have been both physically and spiritually exhausting, and private prayer was the means by which Jesus was refreshed.

The disciples' boat journey proves difficult as they battle an adverse wind. The account of Jesus walking on the water towards them is, again, something we cannot attempt to explain. To suggest that he was walking on a sandbank or surfing on a turtle is banal. Once more, we must ask about the primary theological significance of this event. Jesus has power over the waters, just as did God in Genesis 1:9–10, 21. Here is another display of divine prerogative in Jesus: he is the Lord of nature. This is a fearful event for the disciples, one that they interpret as a phantasm, but Jesus' words are not only meant to reassure them that the phantom is he, and so they need not fear. 'I am he' translates the Greek 'I am'. These words are frequently used by Jesus in John's Gospel: they translate the name of God recorded in Exodus 3:14 in Moses' definitive encounter with the God of Abraham: 'I AM WHO I AM'.

The connection of these words with the nature miracle is an indication that Jesus identifies himself with I AM and sees himself as an expression of this God. Like the title Son of Man, then, which transforms a term simply meaning 'human being' into a title of so much greater significance, the words 'I am' carry greater weight within the context of unfolding biblical revelation. They confront us once more with the mystery and wonder of Christ's person and with the appropriate response that we are to offer to him. In a previous but similar incident, the disciples have cried out, 'What sort of man is this, that even the winds and the sea obey him?' (8:27). Now they have their answer.

# 6  Peter all at sea

Matthew 14:28–36

We might be tempted to see the final words of this week's readings as a comic interlude or a joke told at Peter's expense. It is certainly difficult to imagine any other political or religious movement depicting one of its chief founding figures as a bit of a clown. As the New Testament represents him, Peter is an impetuous figure who often falls over himself in his eagerness to please.

Behind this incident, backed up by others, there must surely lie some genuine historical reminiscences. Those who might harbour doubts as to its historicity might consider that Peter's personality is nonetheless accurately sketched for us here. Seeing Jesus walking on the water, Peter wants to have a go too. Jesus encourages him and, for a few steps, it all works. Then Peter feels the wind and his confidence wavers. Jesus saves him from drowning but admonishes him for his lack of faith. By now, however, the disciples as a group are having their questions answered. They worship Jesus and confess him to be the Son of God. They have come to a significant place in their appreciation of Jesus.

By now, the whole group is back on the north-western shore of Lake Galilee and the crowds are privileged to see the Son of God at work again. They bring him their sick companions, and Jesus is tireless as he deals with them all. The suffering ones are brought to him that *they* might touch *him* (not he them, an interesting reversal). Some can reach only the fringe of his cloak, but for all of them this proves to be enough. All who do so are healed. Such is the power of the Son of God at the height of his popularity.

Jesus' power comes from God by virtue of the Spirit with whom he was endowed in his baptism and who has continued to uphold and empower him ever since (12:28). This is a marvellous man who is full of compassion, tenderness and creative power. There is much in the career of Jesus that the Gospels have yet to tell us, but even at this point we stand amazed at the awesome figure of Jesus the Galilean.

# Guidelines

What we have read of Jesus should bring us to a place of deep personal devotion to him. It is right to worship him, since, although he is truly and fully human, as we are, he is also the incarnation of God in a way that we are not. Although Matthew does not develop his understanding of the person of Christ to the extent that John's Gospel does, the narratives that he records and the titles by which Jesus is addressed are accumulating. Soon there will come a major breakthrough at Caesarea Philippi, when Peter will articulate a serious insight that Jesus will attribute to revelation from God (16:13–20). Jesus is the Christ, the Son of the living God. Because Matthew's account has already stressed these ideas, we are slightly ahead of Peter at this point. We know more about Jesus than the disciples have yet worked out. Jesus now calls us, as he called them, to discipleship, to both believing in him and following him closely in life.

In some church traditions, although the whole of the Bible is venerated, the Gospels are venerated in particular. In certain liturgies, for instance, when it comes to the Gospel reading the New Testament is carried into the body of the church. The people turn to face it and then it is read. This indicates that, although all of scripture should be heeded, the close details that the Gospels give us of the birth, life, death and resurrection of the Lord have a definite priority. If we are to give ourselves to his service and discern where he is at work, we need to absorb everything to do with him in the Gospels. Closeness to Jesus will form and shape us to the point where we might be able instinctively to do what he would do. To claim to know exactly what Jesus would do in the complexities of the present day is pretentious, but the aspiration to be like him is a noble one and no Christian should ever be ashamed of making it their ambition.

**FURTHER READING**

Amy-Jill Levine and Marc Zvi Brettler (eds), *The Jewish Annotated New Testament*, Oxford University Press, 2011.

Leon Morris, *The Gospel According to Matthew*, Eerdmans, 1992.

Tom Wright, *Matthew for Everyone, Part 1: Chapters 1—15*, SPCK, 2002.

# Isaiah 49—55

Isaiah 40—55 clearly addresses the situation of the community that had been exiled from Judah to Babylon by King Nebuchadnezzar in 597 and 587BC (see 2 Kings 24—25). There is quite a difference, however, between chapters 40—48, which refer to the immediate political situation in Babylon as Cyrus the Persian approaches, and chapters 49—55, which seem to look on the situation from a slightly more detached standpoint, with a greater emphasis on the people of God as Zion and as Servant. Equally, there is no longer any treatment of the danger of idol-worship, no reference to the 'former things' and the 'new things' that dominated the earlier chapters, and no direct references to Cyrus or to Babylon. Furthermore, the poems tend to be longer and more reflective than in the previous chapters.

This does not make the appeals any the less urgent; nor is the emotional impact diminished. In reading, however, we have to take different styles into account, in order to ensure that our interpretation is faithful to the text. It is a mistake to confuse poetic vision with the propaganda of close political engagement. Both may express divine truth but it needs to be unearthed in a manner that is appropriate for the material as written.

In Isaiah 49—55 we find some of the best-known passages in the whole of the Old Testament, but, when read with close attention, they sometimes turn out to be a good deal more allusive than is often supposed. It is important, in serious daily study, to try not to bring presupposed notions to the text but to pray for openness to the new things that may broaden our minds and challenge our level of commitment.

Comments are based on the New Revised Standard Version of the Bible.

17–23 November

## 1 A light to the nations

Isaiah 49:1–6

Earlier in this central part of the book of Isaiah, God has already stated that one of his purposes is to bring light to the nations (42:6) and to see his salvation extended to the ends of the earth (45:22). That remains the case here as well (v. 6), but the task of implementing his purpose is now transferred to a new servant. In 41:8–10, and so also in 42:1–4, the servant of the Lord was clearly the faithful people, but now it looks as if God is commissioning an individual (or perhaps a small faithful group) to pick up the baton. Previously, this character was charged with ministering to Israel (vv. 5–6a), but now a more universal task is also entrusted to him.

By what great scheme or plan of action is this universal deliverance to be achieved? What managerial skills will be needed, or what mission statement should be drawn up? Astonishingly, nothing is said about such things. All that happens is that the servant addresses the remote parts of the world (v. 1) and tells them how he has come to have this new role. To use old-fashioned language, he gives them his testimony. It includes his formation as an individual character (v. 1b; compare Jeremiah 1:5 and Galatians 1:15 for this kind of language; incidentally, it was used of the nation of Israel in 44:2, so it does not have to imply an individual), his equipping by God with powerful speech (v. 2), and his designation or ordination to the task (v. 3). So far, then, the servant himself has done nothing.

When he tried to act, he was disappointed and regarded his ministry as more or less a failure (v. 4). Knowing, however, that success depended on his 'cause' being 'with the Lord', he sees that God has rewarded his apparent failure with an even larger task.

In God's work, it seems, who we are matters more than what we do. Activity has its proper and important place, of course, but our more lasting influence will follow from the extent to which the light of Christ shines through us. Jesus himself fulfilled this passage in that sense, even before his adult ministry began (Luke 2:28–32); may our testimony be the same.

# 2  Widow Zion

**Isaiah 49:14–23**

In Isaiah 49—55 there is a regular alternation between poems by or about the male figure of the servant of the Lord and poems by or about Zion, depicted as a female. She is mostly in some distress, as in today's passage, although her fortunes take a turn for the better later on.

This pattern is quite different from what is found in chapters 40—48. There, the audience was regularly addressed as Jacob/Israel, and, although it too was in a dispirited condition, it was meant to be the agent whom God would use for his wider purposes. Zion, though mentioned once or twice in those chapters, was far from a major player. In the present section of the book, Zion rises to the fore, but more as the recipient than as the agent of God's deliverance.

There are, no doubt, some historical factors that help to account for this change of perspective, but they are beyond our recall. At that level, we might suppose that the previous chapters were addressed to the Jewish community in exile in Babylon, whereas in these chapters the focus shifts to the community back home in Judah.

More important than historical reconstruction is the power of the poetic imagery that Zion evokes. She is depicted as a widow, bereft not only of her husband but also of her children. Read again through today's passage with that picture in mind and note how God responds to her distress with a tender empathy. He compares himself to one in a similar condition and shows how her very distress indicates that he in turn could never abandon her (v. 15). He draws on other images, such as the architect and builder (vv. 16–17), to offer further reassurance. Best of all, however, he promises that Zion's children (presumably those returning from the exile) will be so numerous as to overwhelm her with the disbelief of surpassing joy (vv. 19–21). Indeed, the oppressive nations will be transformed into the agents and servants of this change of fortune (vv. 22–23).

The poetry is, of course, visionary—things never worked out quite like this—but a sense of vision can influence us powerfully in positive directions. It might not be too fanciful to compare Widow Zion with the New Testament's Bride of Christ, to find a way of applying this imagery to the situation of the Christian community in ancient times and today.

# 3   A listening ear

Isaiah 50:4–9

This short passage falls into three obvious sections. In the first (v. 4), the speaker (could it be the prophet himself?) reflects on his experience of willingly listening to God's word. This is his daily delight, and, unlike the earlier generation (see 30:8–9), he does not rebel against it. Rather, he finds it to be the source of his own sustaining ministry. Just like Isaiah's own closest associates (see 8:16), he is a 'disciple' (misleadingly translated 'teacher' by NRSV) in the best sense of the word—one who learns in order to be able to serve.

This is far from universally appreciated, however, and, as was the experience of our Lord himself as well as many of his followers, there are those who violently reject him (vv. 5–6). Rejection can, sadly, still be violent in our world today, although in many societies it now takes more sophisticated forms. Such rejection of the message has an effect on the messenger and can be personally damaging. It is no use pretending that discipleship and universal popularity will ever be seamlessly coupled.

The rejection is met, finally, by a combination of determination, which must be based on the daily meditative discipleship from which the passage started out, and a settled assurance that vindication may be left in God's hands (vv. 7–9). It is an insightful foretaste of the triumphant words that bring Romans 8 to a close (vv. 31–39): 'If God is for us, who is against us?' This is not a mindless triumphalism, seeking to gain its victory by superior force, but rather an inbuilt confidence in God that can lift us above the very real and often hurtful rejection that we currently experience, in pursuit of something with more lasting and sustaining value.

# 4 Righteousness in the heart

Isaiah 51:1–8

These verses are the first part of a long poem that stretches as far as the beginning of chapter 52. See how neatly it is constructed! In today's verses, three paragraphs are introduced with the command 'Listen to me' (vv. 1, 4, 7), although the middle one of these three actually uses a different word in the Hebrew. Then we find three paragraphs in the longer second part, starting with 'Awake, awake' in 51:9 and 52:1 and the very closely related but slightly different 'Rouse yourself, rouse yourself' in 51:17.

In both parts of this poem, an important theme to trace is the way that good religious desires become 'internalised'. That is to say, there is some process by which the things we think we need to chase after turn out, by God's grace, to have been within us all along. In verse 1, accordingly, we find the people being addressed as those who 'pursue righteousness', who 'seek the Lord'. By verse 7, however, they have become those who 'know righteousness' and 'have my teaching in [their] hearts'.

How do they get from A to B? They are urged to reflect on several of the fundamental building blocks of their faith—the lessons learned from their early history, which show how God can transform people whose circumstances seem to have no potential (vv. 1–2); God's promise to do the same for desolate Zion (v. 3); a reaffirmation of his intention to use this transformation for universal illumination (vv. 4–5); and a reminder, as so often in the preceding chapters, that he is the creator whose deliverance is even more enduring than the created order (vv. 6, 8).

There is a natural human tendency to crave the new and unfamiliar, and, of course, that has its necessary place. At the same time, however, all exploration should be accompanied by a firm reliance on God's prevenient grace, meaning that our discoveries are of truths that are already there, even if hidden or forgotten in the meantime. God's word has drawn near in Christ, and our attitude should therefore be one of accepting the truths he offers, not seeking to grab at things which turn out to be nothing more than the invention of our own minds.

## 5 Rouse yourself, Jerusalem!

Isaiah 51:17—52:2

The pattern that we saw yesterday in 51:1–8 is repeated to some extent in the present passage. The whole section begins really at verse 9, where the people urge God to 'awake' and 'put on strength'; at the end, however, he replies, 'Awake, awake, put on your [own] strength, O Zion!' (52:1). Thus, like righteousness yesterday, so with strength today: there is some process whereby we find that we have what we thought we lacked.

The people could hardly be blamed for feelings of complete weakness. Isaiah 51:17–20 describes in vivid and painful detail how much Jerusalem suffered in its fall to the Babylonians, and this suffering is interpreted shockingly as the result of having to drink to the dregs the cup of God's wrath. It is a terrifying scenario that leaves Jerusalem devastated and destroyed, famished and bereft of all her 'children'. There is apparently none to comfort her (v. 19), a theme that is repeated in the book of Lamentations. What else can she do but implore God to awake to renewed acts of deliverance, as in previous times?

With an unmerited grace that defies logical explanation, God responds that he is about to turn the tables on Zion's oppressors, making them suffer the fate that they have administered to her under his direction (vv. 21–23). The result will be not only that Zion gains the strength to get up (52:1–2) but that she will do so as a newly decked bride in resplendent garments, with bonds loosened and dust shaken off. In this collage of images, she will no longer be raped by the uncircumcised and unclean but, we may infer, will be kept pure for her legitimate bridegroom.

Few passages show more forcefully how God's deliverance is unearned, unexpected, and far surpassing any reasonable expectation. This does not mean that the suffering that precedes it is not deep and dark; the war-crimes alluded to here are real and, sadly, still familiar in today's world. They may serve as a cipher for other forms of oppression and grief as well. Beyond them, however, lie the promises of God for Zion's blessing, which ultimately will prevail; and in Christ God has made those promises real in even greater measure. 'Amazing grace' is the only appropriate response.

# 6 Your God reigns

Isaiah 52:7–12

In some ways, these verses form the climax to the passage that started in chapter 40. Verse 7 echoes 40:9, for instance; the nations openly 'seeing' God's salvation (v. 8) reminds us of 40:5, and the theme of God 'comforting' his people (v. 9) reflects the opening words of 40:1. So, if verses 7–10 sum up the best of what has gone before, they serve now also as the build-up to the climactic command to depart and go out from Babylon at the start of the great journey home—not just the return of the people alone, but also of God himself (v. 8) as Zion's own king. This is what we have been waiting for throughout the previous chapters.

At this point the prophet draws very clearly on the description of the first exodus, the escape from Egypt under the leadership of Moses. At each point, however, he indicates that the present journey will be even more wonderful than the previous one. The first exodus was undertaken 'in haste' (a rare word in the Old Testament) as the Israelites fled Egypt (Deuteronomy 16:3; see also Exodus 12:11), but this time 'you shall not go out in haste' (v. 12). Even better, in the first exodus the pillar of smoke by day and of fire by night showed the people the way and guarded them against attack from the rear (Exodus 13:21; 14:19–20), whereas now it is God himself who will fulfil these roles in person. The 'vessels of the Lord' (v. 11) are presumably those that were taken away from the Jerusalem temple when it was sacked by the Babylonians, and their return is vested with considerable significance in the restoration narratives (see, for instance, Ezra 1:7–11). In the first exodus, only religious specialists were allowed to carry the sacred vessels (Numbers 4) but now this command is issued to all the people, so long as they are prepared. In many ways, then, this exodus will surpass the first exodus.

The insight of faith is needed to see modern political and social issues in terms that reflect previous experience of God's ways; the present always seems so humdrum in comparison. We need to heed the voice of Christ, who gives us a new commandment to love (John 13:34) and promises ultimately to 'make all things new' (Revelation 21:5).

## Guidelines

The passages we have read this week include some of the finest poetry in the Old Testament. The prophet was clearly inspired, by the intensity of the message he wanted to deliver, to do so in an aesthetically attractive manner. It is therefore very pleasant to read, and, assuming that we have a broad sympathy with the Bible, is likely to inspire us as well.

The question this raises for us, as we seek to interpret and apply the passages, is the suspicion that sometimes the poet has allowed himself to be carried away and even to exaggerate his point. The history of the return from Babylon to Judah was not nearly as glorious as we might suppose from these chapters, even if some who undertook the journey were encouraged to do so by hearing or reading this material.

So the questions we need to ponder now are: does it matter if the Bible is sometimes unrealistically exaggerated? Is there still a place in our

Christian service for visionary exhortation and motivation? How can we bridge the gap between scriptural vision and the humdrum nature of day-to-day living? How should we set about interpreting the Bible in a way that remains true to its vision but is also grounded in real experience?

These are far from simple questions! Reflection on them may be helped by a consideration of the place of great art and music to extend our human imagination and to 'improve' our outlook. To ignore the questions runs the risk of leaving the Bible behind in a museum of curiosities.

# 1 See, my servant

Isaiah 52:13—53:3

Over the next three days we shall be working slowly through one of the best-known passages in the Old Testament, allowing time to reflect on it fully. Many of us, of course, immediately see it as a prefiguring of Jesus in his sufferings on our behalf, whether because of its use in the New Testament or because we cannot escape the echoes of Handel's *Messiah*.

While there is legitimacy in approaching the passage in that way, the disadvantage is that it then cannot tell us anything fresh or unexpected. We know the answer, so to speak, and we read in such a way as to make each part match up, whether it fits comfortably or not.

I therefore invite you to read it this time from a different perspective, namely that of the people who must have heard or read it for the first time, centuries before the coming of Christ. How, in the light of the part of Isaiah we have already studied, could they have understood it? I do not for one moment suggest that my reading is the only possible one—scholars are very divided about the interpretation of this passage—but I offer it as one approach among several that could be helpful.

We note today that the passage starts with an emphatic assertion that God will vindicate his servant in such a way that foreign nations and their kings will marvel at the change in his fortunes (52:13–15). This sounds just like the message we have already heard several times, about the universal reaction to God's deliverance of his people. Given that the servant was clearly 'Israel' earlier (see, for instance, 41:8–10), perhaps we could read this passage as a reflection on the sufferings of the people in exile and the universal benefits that will follow from their deliverance.

The amazement of the kings at what they are witnessing is then given expression in 53:1–3 (and beyond). This group of exiles was despised and rejected, without any promise or potential in their situation. We shall see more of that tomorrow, but for the moment we can simply recall that God can indeed choose 'what is low and despised in the world… to reduce to nothing things that are' (1 Corinthians 1:28).

## 2  He has borne our infirmities

Isaiah 53:4–6

These verses record a dramatic transformation in awareness. Assuming the speakers still to be the kings of other nations, they have naturally thought that the one in view—the exiled Judean community—was suffering through its own fault. This is the way we all think initially when we see somebody getting into serious trouble. 'He had it coming to him'; 'She's got what she deserved'; such sentiments are heard all the time in the press and in informal conversations in the pub or over the garden fence. And in the ancient world, if perhaps not so commonly now, it can all be put down to the agency of God (v. 4).

The complete *volte-face* that follows gives an indication of the devastating surprise that the change in the servant's fortunes has occasioned (52:15). It is not *his* sins, transgressions and iniquities that have caused his diseases, infirmities and bruises, but 'ours'. It is not often we hear politicians talking like this! What is more, this servant has suffered far more than he directly deserved (see 40:2), so we can now see that it was God's way of dealing with our iniquity through him (v. 6).

The witness of this servant of the Lord, as of every such servant, is thus genuinely life-changing. But what has the servant said or done to bring it about? Nothing. No word of his is recorded. In fact, all the action throughout this chapter concerns what has been done to him by God or by others; not one single action of the servant is recorded. This is a pattern of witness that is foreign to much of the church, where members are assessed by the amount of activity they put in. Nor can we construct much of a theory of atonement out of this passage; the saving change of attitude comes about as the result of seeing how God has accepted the servant while all others reject him. The silent servant, apparently resigned to undeserved rejection and suffering, achieves more by allowing God to use him in this mysterious way than any one of us has ever done by just being busy.

## 3  He shall see light

Isaiah 53:7–12

Some of the Hebrew in these verses is difficult, and the various English translations differ in some details from one another. We must be careful in this chapter, therefore, not to build too much on some individual detail here or there. The basic outline is clear enough, however, so we may proceed on that basis without hesitation.

The present verses start from where we left off yesterday—with the servant's total silence (v. 7)—but they move swiftly on to the low point of an unjust arrest and sentence and the unwarranted death of the servant (vv. 8–9). This situation may be closely compared with Ezekiel's vision of dry bones (Ezekiel 37), a chapter that comes from very much the same circumstances as this passage in Isaiah. Just as, there, the bones of the whole house of Israel were very dry but were miraculously raised up so that 'they lived, and stood on their feet' (Ezekiel 37:10), so here the crushed, executed and buried servant will live again, will prolong his days, will see his offspring, and will enjoy a portion with the great. The poem therefore ends by returning to its starting point, with the servant exalted by God (see 52:13). It adds, however, a closing reminder (53:12) that it was in this way that the sin of many was borne away.

If I have been right to see in this poem a profound theological reflection on the experience of exile, that does not by any means remove it from the circle of Christian experience. We learn, perhaps, that there is a great deal more to the work of God through his servant than simply tracing one-to-one equivalences with scenes from our Lord's passion. There is a pattern laid out here of which he was indeed the supreme fulfilment, but we do well also to remember that when this passage is quoted in the

New Testament, it is in the context of an exhortation that in his suffering Christ left us 'an example, so that you should follow in his steps' (1 Peter 2:21). As well as telling us about Christ, the passage should tell us about ourselves, not so much as individuals but as the servant people of God, together, on earth today.

# 4 Great compassion

Isaiah 54:1–10

Once again our attention is switched from the male character of the servant to the female figure of Zion. As before, her condition starts as one who is in desolation, widowed and bereaved of her children. In the previous chapter, the servant's suffering resulted in widespread blessing for many outside the community of God's people. Here, we see how Zion's condition too is transformed. It is not certain how servant and Zion should be related, but it is clear that any Judean reader would have readily identified with her as depicted here.

With some poetic licence, the one who is widowed and has not been in labour suddenly finds that she now has more children than she did when she was married! No wonder she bursts into song (v. 1). She will need to make large extensions to her residence to accommodate them all (presumably a depiction of those returning from Babylon: vv. 2–3), and the following verses continue to express her newly restored condition.

This background may help us to understand what then looks like a contradiction in the text. Having been told since 40:2 that Israel's and Zion's suffering has been double what was deserved, with long passages in which their dispirited condition has needed to be addressed, we now suddenly find God saying that he abandoned them only for 'a brief moment' (vv. 7–8). Does this trivialise the years of suffering, whether in Babylon or in Judah? Far from it; the point of the rhetoric here is not to minimise the pain but to extol the magnitude of the deliverance. Just as Noah's flood was devastating but time-limited and never to be repeated (vv. 9–10), so will be the past decades of exile and abandonment. With hindsight, the new condition will put even those years into perspective and lead to a fuller appreciation and deeper sense of God's compassion.

It is hardly the height of pastoral wisdom to say to one who is suffering that things will look better later on. However, an increasing appreciation of the benefits of Christ's passion will help us to appreciate God's compassion more deeply. Thus we may be enabled better to weather the storms of adversities that are ultimately temporary, however severe they feel. It might be helpful to read 2 Corinthians 4:7–18 alongside this passage to see the underlying truths expressed in overtly Christian language.

# 5 Wine without price

Isaiah 55:1–5

It looks as if this passage starts off with the most colourful of images—the ubiquitous water seller in the oriental bazaar, calling out for custom. His cries can bring welcome relief on a hot afternoon, and we cannot begrudge him the pittance that he asks for a drink from the carrier on his back. Here, however, his role is parodied: no money need be paid for the food and drink that are offered, and they are a good deal richer than just water. Furthermore, the satisfaction from the provision will endure; this is no invitation to a passing fancy.

What is it, then, that is offered so freely? The secret lies in the words 'Listen carefully to me' (v. 2), which are amplified in verse 3. This goes further than just a promise of blessing if the listeners agree to return to Zion. Rather, as they do so, the promise that was once vouchsafed to David will be transferred to them all. Specifically, the leading role that he played internationally will be picked up once again; just as, through his conquests, he became a witness to the greatness of God in his day, so this despised community of exiles will find their situation transformed. They too will become an attractive witness to the nations, who will come running to them for illumination because of the way God has 'glorified' them.

It is clear that this is really a summary of much that has gone before, but set out in such a way as to encourage a cheerful response. We might not think that is necessary, but it was—and it still is. Many of us have difficulty in accepting that what God has done for us is 'free at the point of delivery'. It is almost demeaning, we argue, not to be asked to contribute something; won't a few extra kind deeds, or a bit more in the collection, gain me some credit? If we think like that, perhaps we have not yet come to terms with the depths from which we need deliverance. The astounding promise of verses 3–5 is way beyond our reach. We could never achieve so much unaided. It is wine, without price!

# 6 Do not procrastinate

Isaiah 55:6–13

God's word was a key theme of the opening verses of Isaiah 40, and it takes centre stage again as we round off this section of the book. 'God's word' here is not to be equated with the Bible as such; most of the Bible had not yet been written! Rather, it is God's powerful word, spoken in creation to order our cosmos, reiterated through this prophet to bring light to those in the darkness of oppression, and ultimately revealed to us in human form in Christ. It expresses more than we can take on board of God's mercy and willingness to pardon (v. 7), and it exceeds what even the most gifted human can conceive (vv. 8–9). Unsurprisingly, it will not be frustrated in achieving God's purpose of fruitfulness and blessing (vv. 10–11).

There is an urgency to the initial appeal in verses 6–7, however. God's word cannot be ineffective, but part of its glory is that it does not force itself on unwilling recipients. 'While he is near' sounds time-limited, and in one sense it is. If the prophet's audience failed to listen and respond straight away, he knew that gradually they would become ever more hardened against the message. It is not that God will ever give up, but that we make it harder for ourselves if we constantly ignore the opportunities to listen. The spiritual return path, just as much as the physical one, lies open, and the prophet makes a final appeal for his audience to take it.

And if they do? What a riot of metaphor awaits in verses 12–13. Do not try to work this out botanically! The depiction of hills and trees absurdly sharing in the exiles' joy is more or less unparalleled, but effective. Such poetry is not there for analysis but for reading aloud, singing and laughing at its sheer exuberance. It comes shockingly soon after the depths of chapter 53. It does not deny the reality of that suffering but affirms that it was not in vain. God's final word is one of joy, no matter which path leads to it, and it is that joy that constitutes his most lasting memorial.

# Guidelines

The chapters we have read this week have swung dramatically in mood from the depths of undeserved suffering to the heights of joy. Still today there seems, at first sight, to be an unfair distribution of experience, whether globally between different parts of the world or in personal terms. Some people seem destined to suffer more than their share of adversity while others seem to breeze through life in a relatively untroubled manner; indeed, it is likely that the readers of *Guidelines* could be split along these lines, while many encounter wide variation over the course of the years.

The passages we have read reflect this experience, and in so doing they also remind us of the life and ministry of our Lord, both in his passion and in his resurrection and glorification. As you consider your own experience in this regard, how far should this variation both prepare you for troubled times and encourage you to remember that suffering can be redemptive and is temporally limited? Do you think that this is just a Christian idealistic escape from reality or does it reflect a major theological truth that should sustain us on our journey?

In chapter 53 in particular we saw that a further burden was rejection by society for the sake of faithfulness to our God-given mission, and of course this can apply to us either as individuals or to the church collectively or in some particular locality. While a sensible first step is always to make sure that the rejection is not because we are making ourselves unnecessarily unpopular for a wide variety of possible reasons, it is helpful also to reflect alone and together on the redemptive, if costly, value of service as salt and light in the world (see Matthew 5:11–16).

Either way, let us uphold in prayer those (perhaps including ourselves) who are currently struggling with this very real dilemma, and 'may our prayer not be made empty by our neglect but carry with it our readiness to act as your servants' (Roger Pickering).

## FURTHER READING

Richard J. Clifford, *Fair Spoken and Persuading: An interpretation of Second Isaiah*, Paulist Press, 1984.

John Goldingay, *The Message of Isaiah 40—55: A literary–theological commentary*, T&T Clark, 2005.

Claus Westermann, *Isaiah 40—66: A commentary*, SCM, 1969.

# Church: a disciple-making community

Matthew's Gospel ends with an extraordinary encounter. A man who died a criminal's death on a cross a few days before appears alive on a mountaintop to eleven of his followers. He tells them he has been given authority over the whole universe and commands them to recruit and train people from all nations to obey all his teachings (Matthew 28:16–20). The Church's 'great commission' is to make disciples.

How effectively are we doing this work for the Lord in and through our churches today? I began thinking about this after we launched the first Messy Church in the parish where I'm vicar. Messy Church is a fresh expression of church aimed at helping families with little or no church background to explore the Christian faith through an experience of a welcoming Christian community, creative activities, celebration and a shared meal. The concept has spread rapidly to churches in many different contexts and countries. People of all ages love coming, but one of the key questions raised by church leaders and others has been, 'Can Messy Church make disciples, or is it just an introduction to the Christian faith?'

I started researching what we mean by discipleship, looking at how Christians set about making disciples in New Testament times and down the centuries, and how we can continue to fulfil Jesus' commission today. I was intrigued to discover that the word 'disciple', while common in the Gospels and Acts, never appears in the rest of the New Testament. Believers are referred to as 'the saints' (meaning 'holy ones'), 'brothers','children of God', those 'who are in Christ Jesus' and 'servants of God', but never 'disciples'. As Alison Morgan, author of the *Rooted in Jesus* discipleship course, succinctly puts it, for the writers of the epistles, 'the plural of disciple is church'. The local church is where disciples are made, the community where they learn and grow together as the body of Christ.

Over the next two weeks, we shall be studying passages from both Old and New Testaments to discover more about discipleship in community.

Unless otherwise stated, quotations are taken from the New International Version of the Bible.

# 1 The first great commission

**Genesis 12:1–8**

God commands Abram to go and be a blessing, promising that 'all peoples on earth will be blessed through you' (v. 3). This is the first great commission in the Bible (Wright, *The Mission of God's People*, p. 41), the launch of God's plan to deal with human sin and heal the nations through a community—Abram's family.

Abram and Sarai are given new names by God in Genesis 17:5–6, 15–16 to affirm that they are the start of a dynasty. This wealthy but old and childless couple from the ancient city of Ur are arguably the prototypes for all disciples. The apostle Paul says that Abraham is the father of all who believe (Romans 4:11–12). For Abraham and Sarah and for us, discipleship begins with God's gracious call. It is not because we are remotely qualified for the job. Through grace we are called to become part of God's covenant community, we are blessed and we are sent out to bless the world.

Abraham responds to God's call with faith. He trusts God's promise sufficiently to drag Sarah and his entire household, including his nephew Lot and all their flocks, herds and servants, off into the unknown. Discipleship involves embarking on a long journey with God. As this journey unfolds in Genesis 12—23, we see God testing and training Abraham's and Sarah's trust and obedience through many trials and troubles. Of course, this is how all disciples are meant to grow in their relationship with God, in trust and obedience, through the hands-on immersive learning experience of life with all its ups and downs, the special memorable moments and the rather dull routine times.

It is heartening that Abraham and Sarah are so evidently far from perfect. Their faith wavers, just like ours. Doubts and fears lead them to make bad decisions that have near-disastrous consequences (see, for example, Genesis 12:10–20), and yet the Lord patiently persists with them, just as he persists with his church as he refines us in the crucible of experience (see Romans 5:3–5 on the positive outcomes of suffering and Hebrews 12:1–1 on the fruits of God's discipline in our lives).

# 2 Desert discipleship training

Exodus 17:1–7

God keeps his promise to Abraham and Sarah. By the time their grandson Jacob moves with his sons and their families to live with Joseph in Egypt, there are 70 descendants of Jacob (Exodus 1:5). They continue to multiply, becoming so numerous that a new Pharaoh tries to control their numbers through slave labour and killing male Israelites at birth. God calls Moses to assist in rescuing 'my people' from misery (Exodus 3:7), and eventually, rather like the US troops during World War II who were taken out into the Mojave Desert to train for combat in North Africa, the Israelites are led by the Lord into the testing environment of the desert of Sinai. There, he will prepare them to be his people of blessing and will give them their 'marching orders' in the form of the ten commandments (Exodus 20).

Fresh in their minds should be their miraculous rescue by God from the pursuing Egyptian army (Exodus 14:19–31). We might expect them to be full of gratitude and ready to trust God and follow wherever he leads them. In reality, they are continually moaning about the lack of creature comforts and wishing they were back in Egypt (16:2–3). The Lord repeatedly supplies the food and water they need, hoping to see them grow in obedience (16:4), but they keep on testing the Lord, and the place names Massah and Meribah become for ever associated with Israel's inability to learn that the Lord is with them (17:7).

What about God's people today? In Hebrews 3:7–19, the writer urges the church community to learn from this story. We are to watch out for each other's attitude of heart (v. 12) and encourage one another every day (v. 13), because we need more mutual support. We must hold on to our confidence in Christ (v. 14), for he is the Rock from which all God's people drink while training in the desert (1 Corinthians 10:1–5).

# 3 Festival and family

Deuteronomy 6

After 40 years of desert training, Moses' final task is to prepare God's people to enter the land promised to Abraham. In effect, this is another commissioning to go and make a community of disciples who will obey all of God's commands for generations to come. How is this to be done? Moses instructs the Israelites to set up a system of festivals and family routines that will constantly remind them to love and obey the Lord.

Families are told to remember and keep talking about the Lord's commandments while going about their daily lives (vv. 6–9). The story of how God rescued them must be told to their children, so that the next generation understand why they should love the Lord and keep his decrees (vv. 20–24). Acquiring these holy habits will prevent them from losing their sense of common identity and purpose among their pagan neighbours. The intergenerational festivals stipulated by the law (Deuteronomy 16:1–16) will bring together the whole community at intervals through the year to commemorate and keep alive the story of what the Lord has done for them and renew their commitment to living as his people.

This all sounds great in theory but, sadly, when God's people entered the land they did forget the Lord and followed other gods. So was Moses' community discipleship strategy flawed, or was it simply never pursued in the right spirit?

A more immediate question for us is, do our daily routines and our annual church festivals help us to remember that we are disciples of Jesus and enable us to pass on the story of our faith to younger generations? I wonder how many of us frequently discuss the teachings of Jesus at breakfast, on the way to work and when we go to bed. What difference would it make if we did? What can we do to make our annual cycle of church festivals—Christmas, Easter, Harvest, and so on—more effective as celebrations that renew our common vision, refreshing our sense of identity and purpose as God's people and our love for the Lord?

# 4 Jesus recruits his crew

**Matthew 4:18–22**

The final scene of Matthew's Gospel tells us that disciple-making is a central theme for Matthew. Here we observe Jesus recruiting his first crew members for this task.

Jesus was different from other rabbis of his time because he selected his pupils rather than waiting for people to ask to join him. Just as it did for Abraham, discipleship for these fishermen began with a call to leave their old life and radically adjust their priorities. They abandoned their boats and followed Jesus so that he could train them to catch people.

Perhaps Peter and the others heard in Jesus' words an echo of Jeremiah 16:14–16, where God says that he will 'send for many fishermen' to catch his people, and then hunters to seek them out and bring them home from all the lands to which they have been banished. Jesus is fulfilling this prophecy, forming a task force to help him gather people into a new community that will be a witness to the dawning messianic age. They are to be the founder members of his disciple-making community.

To emphasise the authority, priority and urgency of Jesus' call to discipleship, both Matthew and Mark omit any backstory about Jesus' previous meeting with these men. John 1:35–42 records that Andrew and Peter first met Jesus in rather different circumstances, but Matthew and Mark focus on the moment when the fishermen literally take a step of faith and start working as apprentices, learning new skills from a new master.

It is helpful to think of discipleship as being apprenticed to Jesus in his disciple-making team, learning from his example and under his direction, but there is one significant and challenging difference between being an apprentice and being a disciple. Apprenticeship usually lasts for a set period, and comes to an end when the learners have acquired the skills needed to branch out on their own, but as disciples of Christ our apprenticeship to Jesus never ends; he is our master for ever.

# 5  Apprentice apostles

Mark 3:13–19

Jesus selects twelve from his wider group of apprentices to be apostles. According to Mark, they are chosen by Jesus for two purposes: 'that they might be with him' and 'that he might send them out' (v. 14). The first phrase suggests the master-and-apprentice relationship that we have already noted. They observe Jesus in action, preaching, healing and casting out demons, and then they are sent out in pairs to have a go at doing the same (Mark 6:7–13). In Luke 10:1–16, Jesus similarly appoints and sends out 72 other disciples on mission, which suggests that his methods are relevant for all disciples, not just apostles.

While Jesus does frequently give formal teaching to his followers (see, for example, Mark 4:10–12), much of their time is spent simply walking with him, chatting over meals, getting to know Jesus, observing him, watching him praying, and picking up his attitudes and values, like children learning from a parent. The term for this mode of learning is 'socialisation'. Then there is the 'hands on' apprenticeship mode, where Jesus acts as the group mentor and the apostles are sent out to practise doing mission, despite the fact that they have little faith and hardly any theological understanding at this stage—lambs among wolves indeed! Jesus sends them out to learn on the job, to be encouraged by seeing God's power at work (Luke 10:17), and to learn from their mistakes (Mark 9:14–29).

Many Christians feel they are badly equipped to live out their faith in everyday life. There is an increasing awareness that we need to grow in our discipleship, but we tend to think of it as an individual, intellectual objective, often pursued by joining a course, reading books or listening to sermons. These things can, of course, be helpful, but they represent formal teaching—just one of the three learning modes that Jesus used. If we are serious about wanting to grow as followers of Jesus, churches need to offer us more opportunities for relational, hands-on, experiential learning.

# 6 Community for a change

Matthew 5:13–14

Paul Tillich (one of the most influential theologians of the 1950s and 1960s) describes the church as 'primarily a group of people who express a new reality by which they have been grasped. Only *this* is what the Church really means. It is the place where the power of the New Reality which is Christ, and which was prepared in all history and especially in Old Testament history, moves into us and is continued by us' (*Theology of Culture*, OUP, 1964, pp. 40–41). In the Sermon on the Mount, Jesus, like Moses in Deuteronomy, rallies and instructs his disciples to be a people whose priority is to live out the values of the 'new reality' of God's kingdom (Matthew 6:33). This is a call to radical living, to be a community that is distinctive and transforms the world.

At Mount Sinai, God set Israel apart to be his nation of priests (Exodus 19:6). They were to represent God to the world and thus become a light to the nations (Isaiah 49:6; 60:1–3). The community that Jesus gathers has the same priestly and prophetic role as salt and the light for the world.

Salt, of course, adds flavour and preserves food. In the Old Testament, salt was also added to the special incense used for worship in the tabernacle, to indicate its sacred purity (Exodus 30:35), and 'the salt of the covenant' was added to grain offerings as a reminder of the permanence of God's covenant relationship with his people (Leviticus 2:13).

So Christ's salty community should stop the rot and make the world a better place. Interestingly, this is what happens in 2 Kings 2:21 when the prophet Elisha throws salt into a spring to 'heal' the water and bring life and fruitfulness back to the land. Christ's community will transform the world with God's love and healing.

The community that shines with goodness, like a city lit up at night by thousands of lights in windows, will see people come to know and worship the Father. 'The Christian community is to bear witness to the life of the future in the present' (Cray, *Disciples & Citizens*, p. 95). If we are to do this, it is vital that we rediscover how to grow as disciples in community.

## Guidelines

Followers of Jesus are chosen and called by his grace to become a special people set apart to bring God's blessing to the world and incorporate people from all nations into God's disciple-making community. To achieve this commission, we need to be learning together as Jesus' team of apprentices, learning to live out before the world the values of God's new Jerusalem, even when we find ourselves still facing the hardships and temptations of the desert. Lest we forget, we need constantly to encourage one another and celebrate and recall our purpose and identity in Christ.

What do you think are the specific barriers that hinder or prevent our churches from being disciple-making communities? Are there things we need to repent of and change? What should be our prayer for the church in today's world?

Although God's people in the Old Testament largely failed to remember to be a light to the nations, God never gave up on them or his promises. In the same way, Christ promises to be with his followers always, until the completion of God's plan.

# 1 The disciple as child

Mark 10:13–15

Jesus frequently has to rebuke and correct his apprentices. They think they are doing the right thing by stopping people from bringing lots of small children to be blessed by Jesus (v. 13): surely it is becoming an annoying distraction from more important work. But when Jesus sees what they are doing, he intervenes indignantly, because this is a serious mistake. The children must be allowed to come to him. The reason he gives in verse 14 is not what we might say today—that children have as much right to be blessed as adults, because people of all ages are loved and welcomed by God. What Jesus says is the children must be allowed to come because they are just the kind of people to whom God's kingdom is open. The lesson for the community of disciples is that we have to be like little children in the way receive and enter into all that God is graciously offering.

We cannot be sure what aspects of being childlike Jesus had in mind here, but the story that follows immediately afterwards in Mark 10:17–27 (and in the equivalent passages, Matthew 19:13–26 and Luke 18:15–30) is connected thematically and sheds light on this episode. The young man who runs up to Jesus has great wealth, which also gives him status and power—the very things that children did not have in first-century Jewish culture. Sadly, he cannot bear to give them up, and so they prevent the young man from receiving God's kingdom with childlike trust.

The child who has nothing to bring, no status or wealth, is the model for the way this young man and all disciples should enter the kingdom of God. I wonder whether we hinder ourselves and children from receiving Christ's blessing by so often sending them out of our church services to be taught separately. According to Jesus, adults have something vital to learn from children. In Matthew 18:1–4, he calls a child to come and stand in the middle of the group of disciples to show what a 'great' disciple looks like. We will learn what true discipleship is only when we welcome the lowest person into our circle and learn to become like them in our trust and dependence on Jesus.

## 2 The teacher's example

John 13:1–17, 34–37

In John's Gospel, Jesus delivers a long farewell discourse to his disciples on the evening before his crucifixion. The disciples are upset and puzzled by it (16:17–18), and Jesus himself recognises that it is too much for them to take in (16:12). He assures them that the Spirit will remind them of what he has said and teach them the truth (14:26).

The way the evening begins, however, is dramatic and unforgettable. Jesus lays aside his robe, wraps a towel around his waist and, taking on a role normally given to the lowest of menial slaves (preferably a Gentile), begins washing the dust from his disciples' feet. For the teacher to do this task for his pupils was deeply shocking. Peter breaks the embarrassing silence to voice their objection (v. 6), but Jesus explains that this is another thing they must experience now but will understand later (v. 7). Through this shocking demonstration of his servant-love to the disciples, Jesus intends to help them understand the even more shocking but necessary act of humble loving service and cleansing from sin that he is soon to accomplish for them through his death on the cross.

Jesus is also giving his servants and messengers (v. 16) a practical example or pattern to follow (vv. 13–17). He has set a new standard measure of love (v. 34). Jesus has shown us what love is, and all his disciples must copy his example by getting our hands dirty in serving one another, even laying down our lives for one another (see 1 John 3:16–20). In doing this, we shall find that we are serving God's mission to the world, because, Jesus says, our loving service to one another will be a universally recognisable sign that we are his disciples (v. 35). Servant-love is the essence of Christian discipleship and demonstrates Jesus' sacrificial love to the world. Sadly, however, churches are not always renowned for their love by the wider community.

This costly and practical servant-discipleship can obviously be modelled, learnt and practised in Christian communities only where people spend time together and therefore know each other's needs, where practical care is given by all to all and Jesus' work with the towel and on the cross is always remembered.

# 3 Sharing in community

Acts 4:32—5:11

Luke is keen to show us what Christian discipleship looks like in a community of believers filled with the Holy Spirit. The infant church, already several thousand strong, is described as being united in devotion to God and care for one another.

This is the second time Luke has mentioned the way members of the church in Jerusalem shared their possessions (see Acts 2:44–45). This is evidence of the Spirit's work in their lives, because it is a voluntary and spontaneous response to the needs of poorer believers (4:34). Here is a community that is seen to be obeying Jesus' new commandment. For Luke, generosity to the poor is a sign that this is the new covenant community, fulfilling the hopes of Deuteronomy 15:4–11 for the eradication of poverty. The generosity of the wealthier believers is strikingly countercultural and shows a radical change of priorities as houses and land that would normally be handed down to their heirs are sold for the benefit of the needy brothers and sisters in the community of believers.

Just in case we think Luke has a rather idealised, rose-tinted view of this young Christian community, he immediately gives us two starkly contrasting stories—a model to follow (4:36–37) and a warning to heed (5:1–11).

While Barnabas voluntarily sells his field and donates all the funds for distribution to the needy, Ananias and Sapphira pretend to give the full proceeds of the sale of their property but keep part of the money back. Why do they do this? Is it that they just want to look good? Are they worried about not having enough cash for their own needs if they give the full amount away? Whatever their motivation, they are being led by Satan, not the Spirit of Jesus (5:3), and are condemned not for their greed (they were free to donate as little or as much as they wished), but for lying to God (v. 4), pretending to be more generous and caring disciples than they really were.

Later in Acts, it is Barnabas, the example of true and generous discipleship, who alone dares to welcome Paul as a brother in Christ after his conversion, introduces him to the apostles as a genuine convert (Acts 9:26–27) and so becomes a key figure in the development of the mission to the Gentiles, the wider sharing of all God's riches in Christ with the world.

# 4 Growing together

Ephesians 4:1–16

As Paul travelled from place to place, preaching the good news of Christ and establishing churches, he too was eager that these small communities should 'remember the poor' (Galatians 2:10), showing love for their brothers and sisters in Christ, whether Jew or Greek, not only in their local fellowship but also in other places where there was hardship. For example, he urged them all to contribute to his collection for the relief of the famine-stricken church in Jerusalem (see 1 Corinthians 16:3; 2 Corinthians 8).

This was not a charitable sideline to Paul's ministry. It was a practical expression of God's plan to reconcile Gentiles and Jews in Christ. It also reflects Paul's understanding of the Church as the body of Christ, which may go right back to his life-changing encounter with the risen Christ on the road to Damascus, when Paul discovered that in persecuting Jesus' followers he was persecuting Jesus too (Acts 9:4–5). From this discovery may flow all Paul's teaching on how we belong together and should live together in unity as the body of Christ, sharing our joys and sorrows and using all our different spiritual gifts for the common good (1 Corinthians 12).

Some scholars argue that Ephesians may not have been written by Paul, but this epistle draws out further implications of Paul's teaching on the body of Christ. The ascended Lord gives grace to each believer so that, as his appointed apostles, prophets, evangelists and pastor-teachers equip all God's holy people to do their bit of service for building up the body in love, so all will come to full maturity together (vv. 7–13).

We are intended to grow in our faith together in community. How can I grow to be like Christ unless I learn to love, live with and forgive my brothers and sisters as they seek to learn to do the same (see 1 John 4:20)?

Moreover, full Christian maturity is corporate, not individual. The church is like a group of dancers whose goal is to perform perfectly together. This not only requires each dancer to have learnt their own steps, but everyone must rehearse and perform together. The church's goal is to be transformed into the living, obedient body of Christ, a sign and precursor of God's eternal plan to 'gather up all things' in Christ (Ephesians 1:10, NRSV).

# 5  All change

Colossians 3:1–17

Visiting and sending co-workers with letters to the churches were the main ways in which Paul and others sought to strengthen and encourage new believers in far-flung churches, and establish right belief and right behaviour in communities led by relatively inexperienced and largely untrained leaders.

Paul did not found the church at Colosse, but he writes to the believers there with a heartfelt concern for their growth in faith and godly living, saying that he has been continually praying for them to grow in their understanding of God's will so that they will be able to live to please him (1:9–10). His letter gives them both doctrinal and practical instruction, the latter flowing from the former.

In chapter 3 he urges them to focus their hearts and minds on 'the things above' instead of 'earthly things' (vv. 1–2), on heavenly truths— the hidden spiritual realities of being in Christ who has died, is risen, reigns and will return. In Christ they have died to their old life; with Christ they have been raised to a new life that will be secure in him until he appears and they share in his glory (vv. 3–4).

These hidden realities about our status as believers become the reason and motivation for cooperating with God in a complete makeover of our attitudes and behaviour, throwing out all our old habits (vv. 5–9) and adopting the style of God's new season (vv. 10–15).

The result of having this godly mindset should be a radically new community as described in verses 11–17. It is made up of an unlikely mixture of people with very different backgrounds, beliefs, status and values (v. 11). Formerly, these people would have been unlikely to have a kind word to say about each other (Scythians, for example, had a terrible reputation for uncouth language and behaviour), but, if they now know that in Christ they are all of equal status before God and one body, they should do away with all malicious speech and anger (vv. 8–9). Instead they should be ruled by the peace of Christ (v. 15), patient with each other and eager to forgive grievances. They will be a disciple-making community as they instruct and train one another to live by Christ's teaching (v. 16).

# 6  Work in progress and wonder of the world

1 Peter 2:4–10

The building imagery in this passage reminds me of the church of the Sagrada Familia in Barcelona. The building was begun in 1882 but is still unfinished. Nevertheless, it is already a designated World Heritage Site.

Peter wants believers scattered across Asia Minor to realise that they are part of God's great building project, a temple constructed of people—a work in progress but already a wonder of the world.

The cornerstone of this building (against which every stone must be correctly aligned to play its part in God's plan) is the risen Lord Jesus, who suffered rejection and death but is chosen, living and precious to God (v. 4). Believers are living stones like him, chosen and blessed by God as we come to him in faith, even though we may face rejection and suffering like our Lord (see 3:14; 4:12–16).

The building is going up. Its glorious design and dimensions can already be seen, and it is certainly open for business, but it is still a building site with all the associated noise, chaos and mess, and it will remain unfinished until every stone has been put in place. Nevertheless, it is already a place where the world can see the presence and glory of God. The living stones (all sorts of people, Gentiles and Jews together, as Ephesians 2:11–22, with its similar temple description, makes clear) are being built together to be all that God's people were chosen and called to be at Sinai (Exodus 19:6)—a holy nation and a royal priesthood (1 Peter

2:5, 9), offering their daily lives and good deeds as a sacrifice to God and declaring the goodness of the God who has saved them (see Romans 12:2; Hebrews 13:15–16).

Believers in Jesus may be scattered in small churches, struggling with temptation, false teaching, growing opposition and the increasing likelihood of suffering and persecution for their faith, but they are encouraged to see themselves as part of God's great building project. As a colony of exiles from God's kingdom, they are called to sing the Lord's song in a strange land (Psalm 137:1–6). They must stamp out selfishness and live out the values of the coming king (vv. 11–12), and (as we saw in Matthew 5:13) when people see this, they will end up glorifying God with us.

## Guidelines

- How important do you think it is for disciple-making to take place in an all-age church community where children are both seen and heard?
- Tertullian, an early Christian apologist, writing in AD197, testifies how amazed the pagan people of his time were by the Christians: 'See how they love one another! … how they are ready even to die for one another!' (*Apology* 39.7). What do we do as Christians that amazes people today? How can we become more recognisably like Jesus?
- What do you think we and our churches need to learn from the generous sharing and common life of the early church in Jerusalem?
- How does your church help you grow in your faith and discipleship? How might there be more opportunity to learn from each other and mature together?
- How can we have a godly mindset and change our old ways for new?
- What do you find most encouraging and most challenging about being a living stone in God's great building project?

**FURTHER READING**

Christopher J.H. Wright, *The Mission of God's People*, Zondervan, 2010.

George Lings, *Encounters on the Edge*, No. 53: Crossnet, Church Army, 2012. See www.encountersontheedge.org.uk.

Graham Cray, *Disciples & Citizens: A vision for distinctive living*, IVP, 2007.

Paul Moore, *Making Disciples in Messy Church: Growing faith in an all-age community*, BRF, 2013.

# Advent (Isaiah 11:1–9)

This week's Advent reflections will offer a rather different approach, in terms of the selection of readings. Each day we will take a verse or two from Isaiah 11:1–9 as well as a longer New Testament passage that seems to echo the thoughts in our Old Testament text.

Isaiah 11:1–9 is one of three well-known passages from the first part of the book that have traditionally been linked to Jesus Christ. The other two are 7:10–17 and 9:1–7.

While earlier generations confidently identified direct references to the coming of Jesus in these and similar passages, in some cases even working out the mathematical improbabilities that all the messianic prophecies in the Old Testament were chance occurrences, as a form of apologetic, there are other ways to understand them.

For instance, we can understand some of the references as ideas that influenced Jesus and that he chose to fulfil: in other words, they became 'prophetic' because Jesus chose to make them so. An example would be Isaiah 61:1–3, applied by Jesus to himself in Luke 4:18–19. Other passages, we might accept, were viewed as prophetic by the writers of the New Testament but would not necessarily carry the same weight for us. (Matthew 2:17–18, presented by the Gospel writer as a fulfilment of Jeremiah 31:15, is often viewed in this way.)

However, the approach we are taking here is different again. I am linking verses from our passage in Isaiah with incidents in the New Testament simply to see how each will illuminate the other. Some of the connections will be more obvious than others, but I hope that all will enrich our preparation for the celebration of the birth of Jesus.

Unless otherwise stated, quotations are taken from the New Revised Standard Version of the Bible.

# 1 A branch will bear fruit

**Isaiah 11:1; Luke 3:23–38**

The prophecy that accompanied Isaiah's great call vision (6:9–13) was a devastating message addressed to Judah, Jerusalem and the Davidic king. Verses 12 and 13 indicated the total destruction of Judah—and yet verse 13 implied some kind of new beginning. A stump of the tree would be left. There is no suggestion of a new shoot from this stump; rather, there is a puzzling reference to 'the holy seed', a remnant that will keep the faith and will survive.

Now, however, in Isaiah 11:1, this stump does offer new life. 'A shoot will come up' and, more than that, 'a Branch will bear fruit' (NIV). Once there is a harvest of fruit, there will be divine approval (see Isaiah 5:1–7), as well as the promise of a new generation of trees from the seed in the fruit. We should not overlook the strong note of judgment in this verse, however. It is not the stump of David from which the shoot grows—rather, it is of his father Jesse. Perhaps because of David's failures, including the murder of Uriah, God has to go further back in order to begin again.

In the New Testament, both Matthew (1:1–17) and Luke provide us with genealogies for Jesus. Although there are many similarities in the lists, there are also lots of differences. I have selected Luke's version as today's reading because it is so stark and formulaic. 'The son of Heli, the son of Matthat...' Drum beat after drum beat is hammered out as the years of history unravel backwards. Unlike in Matthew's version, nothing is highlighted or differentiated as Luke travels all the way back to 'the son of Adam, the son of God' (v. 38). Thus we can see that the point of Luke's genealogy, the 'root' to which it is taking us, is the divine initiative. I would suggest that this is also the point of Isaiah's prophecy. The stump and the fruit-bearing branch may seem like aspects of a natural process, but they involve God's gracious initiative and nurturing all the way through the generations from Jesse to Jesus.

# 2 The Spirit of the Lord will rest upon him

Isaiah 11:2–3a; Luke 3:21–22; 4:14–22

We could spend all week reflecting on the attributes of the Spirit listed by Isaiah and their reflection and amplification in the life of Jesus, but two general comments must suffice. First, we are not meant to miss the link back to the names in Isaiah 9:6, words that probably replay themselves in our minds to Handel's music from *Messiah*.

Second, we should note that these attributes are very appropriate for a monarch. They are exemplified in Solomon, who sought wisdom above all things, according to 2 Kings 3. They also relate clearly to the wisdom tradition, as we see often in the book of Proverbs (especially 3:3–15). One way to understand the origins of Proverbs is to relate it to schools for people being trained to serve in the royal courts.

However, the monarchs of Israel (even Solomon) do not often seem to have matched this ideal, and 'the Spirit of the Lord' is less frequently associated with monarchy in the historical accounts than in the wisdom writings. The exception is Saul (see 1 Samuel 10:9–11). In this episode, Saul demonstrates his connection with the past rulers, the judges, on whom, we are told, from time to time 'the Spirit came'. With the judges, the coming of the Spirit of the Lord seems to have been transitory and given for a specific task (see, for example, Judges 3:10; 14:19). In Isaiah's vision, however, the Spirit 'rests' on the recipient—that is, the Spirit remains on him, without becoming the recipient's possession.

It is Luke who picks up the themes of the growing wisdom of Jesus and the positive responses of people to him because of it (see Luke 2:40, 52). Luke also connects Jesus with the Spirit of God, not only in his origins (1:35) and in his recognition by people like Simeon (2:28–32) but also at his baptism. We can note in passing that it is John who emphasises the Spirit as resting and 'remaining' on Jesus (John 1:32–34).

It is with Jesus' own announcement of his mission in Nazareth (Luke 4:14–22) that we see a shift of emphasis regarding the role of 'king' that Jesus fulfils. Here the emphasis is not on his own spiritual attributes but on his divine mission to the despised.

# 3 He shall not judge by what his eyes see

Isaiah 11:3b; Luke 7:36–39, 48–50

In the British legal system it is the responsibility of the jury to decide the guilt or innocence of the accused only on the basis of what they hear and see—the evidence. So, initially, it is feasible to consider the function of Isaiah's king as that of distorting the evidence by ignoring what he sees and hears, maybe in favour of those who are rich enough to pay bribes or those who are influential in other ways. The fact that such behaviour is criticised in Proverbs suggests that it was probably fairly common.

Of course, this is far from Isaiah's meaning. More appropriately, we can recall the story of Solomon and the two mothers (1 Kings 3:16–28), in which there was no clear evidence, or the story of Joseph, who lived his life not on the basis of what he saw with his ears and eyes but in the light of God's purposes and the dreams he was given. Isaiah's king, unlike King Ahaz (see Isaiah 7:1–17), will not make his decisions in the light of military intelligence or political expediency but in the light of the 'signs' he perceives from God and with the insight that God's Spirit brings.

With such wisdom, Jesus saw through the trickery of the questions that the Pharisees brought to him, just as he saw through the trickery of Satan in the temptations. But if we wish to see Jesus' potent insight at work, I can think of no better illustration than the encounter with the woman who anointed him in the home of Simon the Pharisee. Jesus understood that this was not a woman trying to seduce him or, as might well have been the case, a woman sent by the Pharisees to compromise him and prove that he was a disreputable person, tolerating and associating with sinful women. This is what his eyes might have told him. Rather, looking behind the evidence of his eyes, he saw a woman in whom God's redemptive power was at work.

Equally, he did not see sitting alongside him the righteous Pharisee, his generous host, Simon. He saw a person who was thinking dark thoughts both about Jesus and about the woman (v. 39), and was able to 'answer' Simon's secret thoughts. Thus he defended the oppressed woman and sought to liberate Simon from his delusions—which were based on what Simon's eyes saw and his ears heard.

# 4 With the breath of his lips...

Isaiah 11:4–5; Luke 7:40–47

The story from Luke that we considered yesterday gives a powerful example of the way Jesus lived out Isaiah's prophecy, as he accepted the gift of the 'sinful woman' who lavished her love on him while defending her from the criticisms of the outwardly righteous Pharisee. At the end of the encounter, he pronounced judgment on her—that she was forgiven. So we see the words of Isaiah 11:4a fulfilled:

*But with righteousness he shall judge the poor,*
*and decide with equity for the meek of the earth.*

But there is another side to the coin, which is revealed by the remainder of verse 4. Anyone who is going to protect the marginalised and powerless will have to deal also with their oppressors:

*He shall strike the earth with the rod of his mouth,*
*and with the breath of his lips he shall kill the wicked.*

So, in judging and defending the 'sinful' woman, Jesus also dealt with Simon the Pharisee. By telling the story of the two debtors, he unmasked Simon's venomous thoughts and proved that he lacked discernment, finally implicitly exposing Simon as one who had not received very much of God's love for him.

The parallelism of the couplet in Isaiah 11:4b is worth pausing over. If we understand this kind of parallelism as providing mutual illumination between the two lines, we can note that the word 'earth' in the first line does not mean the physical world (although the prophets and apocalyptic writers often did portray God's judgment on the earth in this sense). The second line makes it clear that 'earth' actually means the wicked people who live on the earth. (In a similar way, John often uses 'cosmos' to mean not the earth or even the universe, but people opposed to God.)

We are also left in little doubt that the weapons of this great destruction are words ('the rod of his mouth... the breath of his lips'). Jesus strikes at Simon's sinfulness through the words of his story. So, in the book of Revelation, John picks up this image and applies it to the glorified Jesus in the form of a two-edged sword coming out of his mouth (Revelation 1:16). Similarly, when Paul uses the metaphor of warfare and weaponry, it is clear that he is speaking not of military but of spiritual power (Ephesians 6:10–13).

# 5  The restoration of paradise

**Isaiah 11:6–8; Revelation 22:1–6**

Today's verses from Isaiah paint a marvellous picture of tranquillity—an image of paradise restored. First we see various segments of the animal kingdom living in total harmony with one another, an image expressed in three parallel lines, each showing a dangerous animal and its harmless prey at peace with each other (v. 6). Then there are two more contrasting pairs of animals, the cow and bear grazing together, and the lion eating straw like the ox. In between, there is the even more touching picture of 'their young', the calf and the bear cub, nestled up together (v. 7). It is tempting to see the breakdown in parallelism here as something that needs emending, but perhaps it also works as a way of rounding off the contrasts.

Verse 8 depicts the restoration of peace between humans and the dangerous animal world. Here, humans at their most vulnerable (the nursing child, in parallel with the weaned child—in our language, the toddler), play with our arch-enemy, the serpent. Clearly this concentration of images is meant to draw our attention to something profoundly important for Isaiah's vision of the future. Yet we search in vain in the Gospels for any indication that Jesus 'fulfilled' this part of the vision, by choice or unintentionally, symbolically or substantially.

We know Jesus was a keen observer of the natural world because of his references to sparrows and wild flowers (Matthew 6:26–28). The Gospels indicate that he even had power over nature, in such miracles as the calming of the storm and the multiplication of the loaves (Mark 4:36–41; 6:35–44). For us, then, living in an ecologically sensitive age, it can be disappointing that Jesus apparently said and did nothing to promote peace in the animal kingdom.

There are (at least) three possible ways to handle this enigma. First, we might say that Isaiah's vision is wrong here, and Jesus rejected it. Second, we could argue that Isaiah intended his prophecy to be taken metaphorically, so we should understand it as a pictorial and hyperbolic way of indicating the comprehensive 'peace' that Jesus came to bring. Third, we might see it as an aspect of the coming kingdom rather than the present kingdom. The book of Revelation, with its description of the new heaven and new earth, moves us in that direction (chs 21—22).

# 6 No more tears

Isaiah 11:9; John 1:1–18

According to Professor Richard Dawkins, the God of the Old Testament is violent and vindictive in the extreme. Isaiah 11:9 suggests something rather different. It envisages God's 'holy mountain' as a place of peace and life, where there will be no hurting or destruction.

Sometimes in the Bible, the 'holy mountain' *is* envisaged as a place of destruction. For instance, in Isaiah 29:1–4 God's own people are to be destroyed in Jerusalem (Mount Zion). Even more frequently it is the scene for the annihilation of those who oppose God's people (for example, Isaiah 29:5–8; 31:4–5). Yet this experience of violence and pain is not God's purpose. We see this more clearly in Isaiah 2:2–4, a prophecy in which international violence becomes a thing of the past as people turn their weapons into agricultural tools to bring fecundity back to the earth.

What is intriguing in both Isaiah 11:9 and 2:2–4 is that the cessation of violence is brought about by 'the knowledge of God'. In 2:2–4 the nations come to Jerusalem to learn of God's ways, and 11:9 includes the beautiful line, 'For the earth will be full of the knowledge of the Lord as the waters cover the sea.' Unlike God's judgement on the earth in the time of Noah, that it was so full of violence that the earth would be covered by the seas, here the seas are in their rightful place and the violence is displaced by the knowledge of God.

The New Testament sees Jesus as the one who makes God known to us (John 1:17–18; 14:6–10). We still look out on a world of violence and pain, but we still look also for the return of the one who, through his own violent death, will one day establish a world of peace and prosperity founded on a profound knowledge of God. Hence we can still celebrate with the angels, singing, 'Glory to God in the highest heaven, and on earth peace among those whom he favours' (Luke 2:14).

## Guidelines

During the past week, we have dissected the picture of the future Saviour which we find in Isaiah 11:1–9, studying it in small sections. It will be helpful to read the whole passage again and reflect on it in its entirety.

There are several approaches we could take:

- Give thanks to God for the different aspects of this vision and for the ways in which the whole of it finds completion in Jesus Christ.
- Consider the passages from the New Testament that you might select to complement this vision of Isaiah.
- Think about and select a piece of music that you consider would enhance this scripture passage as, perhaps, it is read in church.

Which feature of this 'prophecy' do you find most engaging? Which is the most disturbing, and which is the most needed in our age?

What aspects of the 'fullness of Christ' do you think Isaiah might have overlooked?

How do you understand this prophetic passage to function? Did it predict what Jesus would be like? Did it shape Jesus' understanding of himself and so contribute to the style of his messiahship? Or does it work in some other way?

Spend time in prayer thanking God for this vision from the past and the ways in which Jesus' life reflects it. Pray for the many Christian organisations who seek to live out one or more aspects of it today.

# Mary the mother of Jesus

Mary the mother of Jesus is an enigmatic figure. The countless depictions of her in art and sculpture, almost always accompanied by the young Jesus, along with the many Christmas sermons describing her as the example *par excellence* of perfect submission to God's will, create an impression of her in our minds that is difficult to shift. She has become a symbol of ideal motherhood and quiet purity—someone who does not rock the boat. This impression does not necessarily come from the Gospels, however. They say remarkably little about her, but the descriptions we do have of her words, actions and thought patterns enable us to build up a different picture of her, as a person—not a paint or plaster model but a flesh-and-blood woman who must have experienced the full range of human emotion in her role as mother and (more importantly, as we shall see) follower of the Messiah.

Luke is the Gospel writer who gives us the most intimate insights into Mary's role. John and Mark hardly mention her, certainly not by name, and, although she appears in Matthew's birth narrative, she is voiceless there, little more than a cardboard cut-out. Perhaps we can assume that Luke interviewed her personally: he claims to have 'carefully investigated everything from the beginning' (Luke 1:3), so it would be surprising if he had not sought testimony from the one person who really was there at the very beginning of the story of Jesus.

In these notes, we shall cover most of the main biblical incidents involving Mary, sporadic and fragmented as they are, but we shall be asking questions more often than finding answers. Our aim will be, by piecing together the evidence, to understand a little more about what it would have been like to be Mary, a girl who was given the astonishing task of shaping the Saviour of the world from birth to adulthood, and was forced to struggle with the direction his life would take after leaving her care. Our study will, I hope, lead us to view her with a renewed compassion, respect and admiration.

Quotations are taken from the New International Version of the Bible.

# 1 Annunciation

Luke 1:26–38

Why was Mary chosen by God as the mother of the Messiah? Surely not purely and simply because she was willing and submissive. If we consider some Old Testament leaders who were commissioned for great tasks, many of them were called by God despite the fact that they were initially very unwilling. Moses was chosen to lead the Israelites out of Egypt even though he pleaded for God to 'send someone else' (Exodus 4:13). Jonah ran in the opposite direction because he did not share God's compassion for the Ninevites (Jonah 4:2), and Gideon gave the excuse of his extremely low position in his family and tribal hierarchy (Judges 6:15). They all resisted the call at first because they had a clear idea of the enormity of the task and their own inadequacies. Submissiveness was not a required character quality for these chosen ones, so why should it be for Mary?

Told by an angel that she is 'highly favoured' by God and has the opportunity to be the mother of a great king in the line of King David, many a naive girl might grab at the chance. Indeed, Mary asks the immediately obvious practical question of 'How?' but seems not to think any further before giving her consent. 'I'm too young; I'm scared; what will my fiancé think?' would all be reasonable responses. She could not possibly know what such a calling would entail for her in the future. Yet her later behaviour suggests that Mary had a wisdom and maturity beyond her years. Perhaps, then, rather than a mark of naivety or submission, her almost immediate agreement is the sign of an adventurous spirit, spontaneous and with a reckless trust in the ultimate goodness of the world. This made her the kind of person who could work in partnership with God.

Might it be, therefore, that God chose Mary because he saw that many aspects of her character and abilities made her fit for the task? He saw that she could be trusted with the shaping of a unique person—a boy who would grow to be the wisest teacher, the most compassionate judge, the most outstanding servant-leader, the most engaging storyteller, and the most fearless and determined follower of his heavenly Father. As his mother, Mary would have the responsibility of nurturing and guiding the development of that person. This awesome task was entrusted to her not simply because she was willing but because, by God's grace, she would be able.

# 2  Magnificat

Luke 1:46–55

This revolutionary song perhaps gives us a clue as to why Mary was a perfect choice as the nurturer of God's Messiah. She already had a deep awareness that his kingdom turns the world's values upside down. In the kingdom that her son would inaugurate, the hungry would be satisfied and the rich disappointed; worldly rulers would find their power annulled, while the 'little people' (Mary herself included) would be given a voice and an influence on world history.

This chimes in with Jesus' own teaching: 'The last will be first, and the first will be last' (Matthew 20:16); 'Blessed are the poor in spirit... the meek... those who hunger and thirst' (5:3, 5–6); 'How hard it is for the rich to enter the kingdom of God' (Mark 10:23). Growing up in the home chosen for him by his heavenly Father, he would have learnt from his mother that God is no respecter of worldly wealth and influence. With those convictions instilled in him, he could fearlessly face down the arrogant religious rulers and even the Roman authorities who supposedly held the power of life and death. He could authoritatively raise up the oppressed ordinary people who came to him in search of healing and sustenance. He knew from his mother's revolutionary spirit what the true values of God's kingdom were.

Mary's song also shows that she had an understanding of her place in history. She stands in a line from 'Abraham and his descendants' (v. 55) to the future generations who 'from now on... will call me blessed' (v. 48). In her mixture of supreme confidence and humility, she recognises and rejoices in the fact that God's work is a long-term project in which each one of his chosen servants has a job to do and then passes on the baton to the next in line. Again, Jesus shows the same awareness. As his public ministry begins, he deliberately takes his cue from the prophet Isaiah

(Luke 4:18–19) and, as it ends, he passes the empowering Holy Spirit on to his disciples (John 20:22). From his mother he has learnt that God's work extends across all generations—that the kingdom is both 'now' and 'not yet' and is growing ever onward until harvest time.

These fundamental building blocks of his ministry are all there in his teenage mother's song. Perhaps she did not realise they were so important, but God saw that they were.

# 3  The shepherds' visit

Luke 2:8–38

The events of Jesus' birth must have been a rollercoaster of emotion for Mary. The enforced 80-mile trek to Bethlehem at the most inconvenient time imaginable, coupled with the failure to find a quiet place to give birth, would have heightened anyone's anxiety levels. She must have been impatient to see the time when God would really 'bring down rulers from their thrones' (1:52), to stop them herding ordinary people around like this for their own financial purposes.

Then a gang of shepherds bursts in on the scene, jabbering about angelic choirs, exhilarated by the invitation to see the Saviour, the Messiah. I imagine that the shepherds' arrival would have been a comfort to Mary, reassuring her that, despite being just one of a band of peasants pushed around the country by Roman bureaucrats, she has not been overlooked by God in the mêlée. He is still with her; he has accompanied her all the way from Nazareth and has shared the joy of the birth with people who were open-minded and open-hearted enough to catch the wonder and excitement of it.

There is a lot of noise and chatter in this passage (vv. 13, 17, 20), but in the midst of it sits Mary, perhaps overwhelmed but peaceful, 'treasuring up all these things and pondering them in her heart' (see v. 19). Is this another reason why God chose her for the job—that she was calm, deep-thinking and acutely alert to the many different currents flowing around her and her son?

There is more excitement some days later, at Jesus' presentation in the temple, as two more strangers supernaturally recognise the baby as the Messiah. Again, the parents 'marvel' at what is said about him prophetically (v. 33). Two potentially troubling things emerge here, however—Simeon's description of Jesus *first* as 'a light for revelation to the Gentiles' and only then as 'the glory of your people Israel' (v. 32), followed by his words to Mary, 'A sword will pierce your own soul too' (v. 35). The angel Gabriel said nothing about either of these future developments; Mary's Magnificat did not touch on these subjects, and the shepherds seem to have had no notion of anything but praise and rejoicing. Simeon brings a sombre warning of upheaval more far-reaching than any of the characters has yet imagined. No wonder Mary needs to 'treasure' and 'ponder' all these things.

# 4 Jesus in the temple

Luke 2:41–52; Mark 6:1–3

There is more for Mary to treasure by the end of the episode in the temple (Luke 2:51). After all the supernatural goings-on in the earlier verses of Luke's Gospel, this one precious snapshot from Jesus' childhood is full of normal human emotions that every parent, I imagine, can identify with— the fear and frantic anxiety of 'losing' a child, the explosion of relieved anger on finding the child ('How could you do this to us?') and the near-teenager's complete lack of concern ('I'm cool; what are you worried about?'). However, not every parent will have experienced finding their twelve-year-old child engrossed in academic debate (whether in theology or engineering or medieval history or contemporary architecture...) with the foremost scholars in the land.

There are the first hints here that Mary is finding herself slightly out of her depth with her extraordinary son. *Should* she have known that he would be easily discovered at home in 'my father's house' (v. 49)? Or is the fact that she did not immediately think of this possibility an insight into the normality of Jesus' upbringing to this point—the skill with which his mother has succeeded in keeping his feet on the ground without stifling his spiritual and intellectual development?

It is interesting that when Jesus preaches at the Nazareth synagogue, 18 years later, his neighbours in his home town take umbrage because they don't expect him to be speaking like a radical prophet. Mary has treasured and pondered the amazing events of his infancy and his escapade at the age of twelve, but she has clearly not gone around bragging of them. There is no sense that Jesus is a spoilt or 'favourite' child, unlike Joseph with his special coat and hate-filled brothers (Genesis 37:3–4). He is merely 'the carpenter', on a par with his younger brothers and the sisters who are 'here with us' (Mark 6:3). His Messiahship is unrecognised, and the idea that he might turn out to be a 'light for the Gentiles' is unthought-of. Indeed, his suggestion that God might sometimes favour the Gentiles is the cause of the crowd's murderous rage (see Luke 4:25–29).

It is Mary who has provided this 'normal' upbringing of a radical son, giving him a balance between everyday humanity and the knowledge of a unique calling from God, which, at the age of 30, he is beginning to reveal.


# 5 'Out of his mind'

Mark 3:20–35

To his family, looking in from the outside (v. 31), it must have seemed as if Jesus had lost the plot. Why was he wasting his time with this crowd of over-demanding countryfolk when he should have had his focus on the throne of David (Luke 1:32–33)? Yet Mary knew that his ministry would be to the hungry and dispossessed. Why is she so worried?

We see in John 7:1–5 that Jesus' brothers were frustrated with his apparent contentment to be out of the limelight. They thought his goal should be 'to become a public figure'—in today's terms, a celebrity. This was the same temptation that Jesus faced after his baptism (Luke 4:9–11): 'Throw yourself down' from the top of the temple; do something spectacular; grab the headlines.

What were Mary's thoughts at this time? Had her younger, unbelieving sons sown doubts in her mind about Jesus' methods? Was their conversation, evening after evening, about how he was 'doing it all wrong'? With that idea lodged, did Mary to start to ponder all the characters in Israel's history who started out with great potential but lost their way? There was Samson, the promised deliverer whose tempestuous nature repeatedly got the better of him and laid him open to manipulation (Judges

13—16). Moses was ultimately denied entry to the promised land because of one silly error made in a fit of impatience (Numbers 20:12). Even David did great feats at first (1 Samuel 17) but set in motion the events leading to the collapse of his own kingdom with a series of misguided actions (2 Samuel 11). Did Mary start to worry about what might happen if Jesus really was 'out of his mind' (Mark 3:21) or even demon-possessed (v. 22)?

We are not told her response to Jesus' refusal to come outside and be shepherded home, but his denial of the special role of the biological mother must have hit hard (vv. 34–35). In Luke 11:27–28, when a woman shouts out, 'Blessed is the mother who gave you birth and nursed you', again Jesus replies, 'Blessed rather are those who hear the word of God and obey it.' He is no longer a child, and the challenge for Mary now is to move beyond a picture of herself as the one whom 'all generations will call… blessed' because of her motherhood and to take up the blessing of being her son's follower, trusting that he knows the way.

# 6  Pentecost

Acts 1:14; 2:1–4

Luke's Gospel mentions Mary by name no more after chapter 2. Having been the star of the early chapters, she fades out at the end. At the crucifixion, Luke shows only a group of anonymous 'women who had followed him from Galilee' watching from a distance (23:49). It is John who places her stoically at the foot of the cross, close enough to hear Jesus commend her into the care of the beloved disciple (John 19:26–27). So she is present to witness the end of her glorious hopes—to see the angel's promises, the shepherds' excitement, the temple scholars' amazement and even the crowds' hunger for his teaching fall into dust. The day when she sang the Magnificat must have seemed an empty dream. All that is left to her is the prophesied sword piercing her own soul.

On Sunday morning, her place at her son's side is taken by other women: it is Mary Magdalene who has the privilege of being the first to meet the risen Jesus (John 20:11–18). We have no record that Jesus made any special post-resurrection appearance to his mother (although, of course, the lack of a record does not necessarily mean that it did not happen). We can only hope that her hiddenness means that Jesus' followers and her own family closed ranks around her to shield her from further grief.

To read, then, that Mary is constantly present in the upstairs room in Jerusalem, along with the other disciples and even with Jesus' previously unbelieving brothers (Acts 1:14), is a joyous relief. Anyone who has done family history research will know the feeling of 'losing' a relative from the records—missing, perhaps, from a particular census—and then finding them again, another ten years older, listed at home together with other family members. There she is! She's come through! After the long years of treasured promise, followed by misunderstanding, temptations to doubt, and piercing grief, Mary would live the rest of her life knowing Jesus' presence with her through the Holy Spirit.

Tradition says that Mary died in Ephesus. If so, by the end of her life she would have seen at first hand her son's kingdom spreading out from Judea, becoming the promised 'light to the Gentiles' and challenging even the mighty Roman empire, bringing rulers down from their thrones and exalting the humble. Her reckless, adventurous 'yes' to the angel had proved to be the best possible decision.

## Guidelines

In the busyness of this Christmas period, can you find time to ponder, as Mary did, the ways in which your calling from God is being worked out?

- How do you respond to a new and surprising call? Perhaps a leap of faith is required, and courage to take on the job in a spirit of adventure. Pray for the right balance of confidence and humility, to fit in with other servants of God who have gone before or may come after.
- Are troubling elements emerging as it becomes clear that God's purposes are more far-reaching than previously imagined? Can you remain open to the personal cost as well as the excitement of God's bigger picture?
- Does your call seem to be going wrong? Pray that you might maintain trust in God's wisdom through perplexing or mundane times of life.
- Are you perhaps nearing the end of the task that God has called you to, with a sense of joy and fulfilment? Praise God for his faithfulness through the years.

# 1 Peter

For hundreds of years in Europe, Christians have lived in a culture profoundly shaped by the Christian story, its values, priorities and expectations. Historians called this culture 'Christendom'. With the benefit of hindsight, we now recognise that this culture was far from truly Christian and was shaped by many other influences, but Christians generally felt 'at home' in Christendom.

This has not been the experience of Christians in many other parts of the world, where minority status, discrimination and sometimes persecution have required a different perspective on faith and discipleship. Nor was it the experience of the Christians to whom Peter's letter is addressed, and increasingly, as Christendom fades, it is not the experience of Christians in Western societies.

We no longer feel 'at home' in the way we once did. The culture gap between church and society has widened. Our language, convictions and practices, already unfamiliar, are becoming incomprehensible or even offensive. Many commentators are using the language of 'exile' to describe this challenging situation, encouraging us to learn from the Old Testament exile literature (including Esther, Jeremiah, Lamentations, Ezekiel and Daniel).

This week's readings pick up the theme of exile but explore a New Testament text. Peter's readers were members of a minority community, whose perceived deviant beliefs and unconventional lifestyle were becoming worrying to the authorities. Persecution was imminent or already happening. Persecution may seem an unlikely prospect for Christians in Western societies, but Peter's letter might help us to pray more effectively for brothers and sisters elsewhere. We could also learn something valuable about living as 'exiles' in a post-Christendom culture.

Quotations are taken from the New Revised Standard Version of the Bible.

# 1 To the exiles

1 Peter 1:1–16

Peter is writing to Christian communities in eastern provinces of the Roman Empire. He calls them 'exiles of the Dispersion', a description that recalls the experience of Jews in the diaspora. They may not be literal exiles from other lands, but they are not fully at home in their surroundings. Their worldview, lifestyle and priorities are different from those of their neighbours, and this is provoking opposition and difficulties.

As exiles, they are facing temptations, which Peter addresses throughout his letter. In this opening section, he urges them *not* to lose hope, *not* to let go of their faith and *not* to revert to old ways of living. Minority communities are prone to such temptations in the face of pressures from the dominant culture. Peter assures them that their destiny is not defined by imperial propaganda but by the revolutionary good news that they have believed. Likewise, exiles in post-Christendom societies need not be seduced or intimidated by idolatrous political or economic claims.

Hope is a major theme in 1 Peter. What grounds did these beleaguered exiles have for hope? Peter reminds them of God's great mercy, the resurrection of Jesus, their new birth, their promised inheritance, God's protection during testing times and the promised return of Jesus to usher in complete salvation. Their faith is being sorely tested, but hope can inspire joy as their imagination is renewed (these notes will indicate ways in which Peter encourages fresh thinking) and they learn to view their situation from an eternal perspective.

This hope is also their inspiration for living as non-conformists, 'sanctified by the Spirit to be obedient to Jesus Christ' (v. 2). Peter urges the believers to be holy, disciplined and alert in their thinking and behaviour, resisting the powerful temptation to slip back into old patterns of living and the persistent pressure to conform to social norms. He encourages them to recognise that they are exiles, dispersed among those who do not believe what they believe, but that they are also 'chosen and destined by God': these are the two realities that will guide their lives and preserve their faith.

# 2 The time of your exile

1 Peter 1:17—2:10

This section of Peter's letter is rich in imagery and Old Testament allusions, which tumble over each other—seeds and sowing, removing soiled clothing, infants and milk, stones and buildings, and references to Exodus, Psalms, Isaiah and Hosea. Peter is apparently working from memory rather than quoting exactly, drawing on texts and themes popular with other New Testament writers.

He continues to urge his readers to live as 'God's own people' during the time of their exile (2:9). He will later write about loving their neighbours and enemies, but first he writes about loving members of their own community. Motivated by their relationship with God as both Father and Judge, by their costly redemption from old ways of life and by the hope that is founded on Christ's resurrection, they are to be not only individually holy but also corporately holy. Their love for each other is to be genuine, deep and mutual—and Peter then lists attitudes and behaviour that must be put away. This is essential if the exile-community is to be mutually supportive in difficult circumstances and to witness persuasively to God's 'mighty acts' of salvation.

Peter nowhere uses the word 'church' (despite the NRSV translation of 5:13); instead, he contrasts *oikos* (household) with *paroikoi* ('aliens' in 2:11). The exiles may have uncertain status in the empire, but they belong to God's household. Adopting phrases used to designate Israel, he assures them that they are God's own people, royal priests in the temple built on Christ the cornerstone, a holy and chosen nation albeit scattered among the nations. Their calling is to offer spiritual sacrifices and to proclaim in word and deed the saving acts of God. But they can only do this if they are built together as 'living stones' into this new *oikos* through mutual love.

What, then, is our primary identity as post-Christendom Christians in the time of *our* exile? In Christendom, loyalty to family, city, nation or empire often took precedence. But as *paroikoi*, what is our *oikos*? How do we behave within this household and transnational nation? How do we express our commitment to other members of the community, locally and globally? How do we proclaim God's mighty acts to others?

# 3 Aliens and exiles

1 Peter 2:11—3:7

Peter now focuses on relationships beyond the exile-community. How are 'aliens and exiles' to behave, especially towards civic authorities, slave-owners and pagan spouses? He urges abstention from behaviour that would invite criticism, honourable conduct to disarm accusers, proper respect for those in authority, and non-violence in the face of provocation. This will not guarantee security but, if their suffering is unjust and borne without complaint or retaliation, they are following Christ's example and will receive God's approval.

In the Christendom era, this text was interpreted in ways that reinforced hierarchical social structures and did not challenge unjust government, the practice of slavery or patriarchal assumptions. 'Aliens and exiles' in post-Christendom read it differently: we note the subversive elements. Authority is to be accepted but not uncritically: some slave-owners are cruel and some pagan authorities are foolish. Wives can hope to win over their pagan husbands, rather than embracing their husbands' religious convictions, as would normally have been expected. Husbands must respect their wives as joint heirs of eternal life. God is to be feared but the emperor is only to be honoured: in fact, since everyone is to be honoured, the emperor's status is somewhat diminished.

Because we are 'servants of God', we are free people who can no longer accord ultimate loyalty to any human authority—but we must not misuse this freedom. Peter's concern is not to advocate grovelling subservience or to endorse fallen human power structures, but to warn against irresponsible behaviour or contentious reactions to mistreatment. In particular, his readers should refrain from abusive language and threatening behaviour. This is partly to avoid unnecessary suffering (if they are going to suffer, better if they suffer as followers of Jesus), but mainly for 'the Lord's sake' and for the sake of their witness.

Post-Christendom, like first-century Asia Minor, is a missional context. As bearers of a strange story that few people around us now know or believe, our lifestyle is significant. Contemporary 'aliens and exiles' are to be characterised by consistent behaviour, self-discipline, limited but respectful acceptance of authority, harmonious marriages and non-retaliation in the face of provocation. We may still be maligned and mistreated, but we can hope that some will be 'won over' and will 'glorify God'.

# 4  Life in exile

Having focused, in the previous two sections of his letter, first on relationships within the exile-community and then on relationships beyond it, Peter here encourages ways of thinking, speaking and acting that are appropriate for followers of Jesus in all areas of life. For the third time he points to the sufferings of Christ as the incentive for such costly discipleship. Peter's theology of the cross includes not only the unique atoning significance of the death of Jesus but also the exemplary nature of his suffering.

The final verses of chapter 3 are fraught with interpretive difficulty. Who are 'the spirits in prison' and what does Christ proclaim to them? What is the significance of Noah's generation? What is the link between this and baptism in Peter's mind, except that water is involved? There is no space to investigate these questions here. However, the framework of the chapter is familiar: Jesus suffered, died, rose again, ascended to heaven and is seated at God's right hand, and this gives assurance to his exiled followers in their sufferings as they 'sanctify Christ as Lord' and refuse to be intimidated or fearful.

Peter is clear about the demands of life in exile, repeating and reinforcing earlier instructions. He writes first about attitudes that are essential if the exile-community is to remain united and mutually supportive—love for each other, sympathy, tenderness and humility. Quoting from Psalm 34 (and probably with Jesus' teaching on enemy-loving in mind), he insists that they must guard their hearts, words and actions if they are to thrive. In their relationships with those who abuse or oppress them, they must pursue peace, refuse to retaliate and prayerfully trust God for vindication. Their good conduct may save them from harm—and if not, they will be blessed despite their sufferings, because of their obedience.

Peter again reminds the believers that life in exile holds missional opportunities. If they live out the hope they have received through their relationship with Christ, their lives will provoke questions. Alan Kreider, a church historian, says that 'fascination evangelism' was a crucial factor in the early church's growth. If the Christians live distinctively, they should be ready to respond to questions, and a gentle and respectful tone is vital. In post-Christendom, too, nonconformist lifestyles, enemy-loving and gracious verbal witness are essential.

# 5 The end of exile

1 Peter 4

Peter continues to develop themes from earlier in his letter—the exemplary nature of Christ's sufferings, the importance of disciplined living, the witness of a transformed lifestyle, the need for loving relationships in the exile-community (which, in a familiar biblical phrase, 'covers a multitude of sins' as forgiveness is exercised freely, v. 8), and the testimony of suffering as a Christian rather than as a wrongdoer. But now he introduces fresh elements into his pastoral counsel, not least his reminder that exile is not permanent: 'the end of all things is near' (v. 7). His theology of the cross is still evident but the focus is now on resurrection, judgement and the Creator's ultimate purposes.

Peter continues to address the issue of actual or imminent suffering, urging the exiles not to be surprised by it or ashamed when abused, but to rejoice in the privilege of sharing in Christ's sufferings. In post-Christendom Western societies, we struggle to accept the normality of the suffering of Christians, but Peter's perspective is shared by other New Testament writers. Suffering Christians are to trust God and live faithfully, not to think that something strange is happening.

Judgement is a major theme in this section of the letter. We will all give account to God of how we have lived. This solemn reality is a warning to persecutors and those who are dissolute, although Peter leaves their destiny to the imagination of his readers. It is also, however, an incentive to holy living and an encouragement to suffering exiles: God will put everything right, turning pain and fear into shouts of joy. Often viewed as a necessary but negative aspect of 'the last things' or the end of exile, the judgement of a good and gracious God is actually wonderful good news! Judgement is not primarily about punishment, despite the predilection of the Christendom church for retributive approaches to justice, but about righting wrongs and restoring harmony to all creation (Acts 3:19–21; Colossians 1:20).

Peter returns in verse 17 to the *oikos* (household) image of the Christian community, in two ways. Judgement, he says, begins with 'the household of God'. The end of exile will involve giving account to God of life in exile, and this will include the use of God-given gifts of speaking and serving. Peter describes the exiles as 'good stewards', household managers who use their gifts to serve other members of the household and bring glory to the head of the household.

# 6 Humility and resistance

**1 Peter 5**

As he did earlier, in this concluding section Peter first addresses specific groups in the exile-community and then exhorts all his readers to show similar virtues. At the start of the letter he introduced himself as an apostle; now he speaks as a fellow elder and co-pastor to those with pastoral responsibility in the community. Like them, he is an under-shepherd, for Christ is the chief shepherd. Their primary task is tending the sheep (echoing Jesus' charge to Peter in John 21), and Peter tells them to do so with pure motives, enthusiasm and humility.

Humility then becomes the dominant theme as Peter encourages younger members of the community to bow to the authority of their elders, quotes loosely from Proverbs 3:34 and urges all members of the community to humble themselves before God and one another. Centuries of Christendom have embedded humility as a virtue in the Western psyche, but in the empire in which the exiles lived it was perceived as folly and weakness. Humility was a distinctively Christian virtue in that era. Is it still today, or is another Christian virtue distinctive?

Throughout the letter Peter has advocated non-resistance in the face of opposition and abuse, but in these final verses he calls for military-style discipline, watchfulness and resistance. At last the real enemy appears—not persecuting civic authorities, unkind slave-masters or intrusive neighbours, but a prowling lion, their adversary, the devil (v. 8).

Behind those who appear to be their enemies is a force of spiritual evil, which is to be resisted vigorously. The New Testament consistently urges non-resistance and enemy-loving towards human 'enemies' but spiritual warfare against the ultimate enemy and his destructive ideologies. Post-Christendom might be an opportunity to recover this perspective after centuries of fighting those whom we should have loved.

The letter ends with a reminder that the exiles are not alone. Their brothers and sisters elsewhere are enduring similar struggles. This challenge to parochialism is pertinent today, lest we forget those who are suffering for the sake of Christ. Finally, there are greetings from individuals and 'she who is in Babylon' (probably a reference to the exile-community in Rome, as 'Babylon' was code for the imperial capital), and an instruction to express their unity with a kiss of friendship. Peter ends as he began, with a blessing of peace.

## Guidelines

This is a challenging letter, calling us to accept our status as 'exiles', allow our imagination to be renewed, be disciplined and united, live distinctively, love our human enemies but resist the real enemy, and seize missional opportunities. It also reminds us to remember brothers and sisters who are suffering persecution in ways that we in Western societies are not. As you pray:

- Ask for discernment and courage to live as nonconformist exiles and resist only our real enemy.
- Ask for grace and wisdom to respond respectfully and humbly when asked about your faith.
- Give thanks for the suffering, exaltation and example of Jesus Christ.
- Pray for the persecuted and suffering church.

**FURTHER READING**
Michael Frost, *Exiles*, Hendrickson, 2006.
Peter McDowell, *At Home in Exile: The journey towards a new paradigm*, Contemporary Christianity, 2012.
Stuart Murray, *Post-Christendom*, Paternoster, 2004.

# Supporting
# Who Let The Dads Out?
# with a gift in your will

For many charities, income from legacies is crucial in enabling them to plan ahead, and often provides the funding to develop new projects. A legacy to support BRF's ministry would make a huge difference.

Who Let The Dads Out? (www.wholetthedadsout.org.uk) has the potential to make a significant impact on the lives of families, churches and whole communities. It is a catalyst enabling effective missional outreach and ministry to fathers and father figures and their children. Its vision is simple: 'Turning the hearts of fathers to their children and the hearts of children to their fathers' (Malachi 4:6).

Starting with fathers and toddlers, Who Let The Dads Out? groups can develop a range of ministry opportunities with these men, with the result that:

- **Families are strengthened** as dads engage in parenting their children and therefore engage better with their partners in the role of parents.
- **Communities are invigorated** as men develop a stronger network of friends within the local community, helping in the process of binding a community together.
- **Christian faith is passed from one generation to the next** as the church engages with fathers, encourages them to explore faith issues and challenges them to teach their own values and beliefs to their children.

Throughout its history, BRF's ministry has been enabled thanks to the generosity of those who have shared its vision and supported its work, both by giving during their lifetime and also through legacy gifts.

A legacy gift would help fund the development and sustainability of BRF's Who Let The Dads Out? ministry into the future. We hope you may consider a legacy gift to help us continue to take this work forward.

For further information about making a gift to BRF in your will or to discuss how a specific bequest could be used to develop our ministry, please contact Sophie Aldred (Head of Fundraising) or Richard Fisher (Chief Executive) by email at fundraising@brf.org.uk or by phone on 01865 319700.

# The BRF

## Magazine

# Messy Church in 2014

*Lucy Moore*

Ten years ago, in April 2004, the very first Messy Church was held at St Wilfrid's, Cowplain, near Portsmouth. We asked its founder, Lucy Moore, for her thoughts on the past ten years and the possible future for Messy Church.

## What were your expectations for Messy Church back in 2004?

When we held our first Messy Church, we had absolutely no idea it would be the start of such a wild adventure and that over 2000 churches would join us in our messiness. We only started it for our own parish families and are still bemused that it's headed off in so many different directions. The original Messy Church is still going strong: I was down on my knees poking birdseed out of the skirting board crevices only last week, after a riotous session with new families exploring baptism and old familiar friends who have been with us all the way through. One eleven-year-old, Phoebe, after belonging to this congregation since she was a baby, has just decided to come on to the leadership team.

## Why do you think Messy Church has grown like this?

I think it can only be God's Spirit wanting it to happen, longing for the church to understand what church is really for. I know that he's worked through the Fresh Expressions movement, with whom we are now happily Associate Partners. Fresh Expressions encouraged churches to risk being church differently, and spread the story of Messy Church across the world before we were in a position to do so ourselves. Also, it's grown through gossip—one Christian gossiping a good thing to another or one family gossiping the good time they've had at their Messy Church to another family and bringing them along to the next session.

I think, too, that an honest engagement with the needs of families outside the church has meant that the church has tried to meet those needs rather than being hampered by trying to get people to 'do church as we do it', and this has also resulted in growth. And of course, BRF's excellent resourcing in the background has meant great back-up for publicity, design, books and all things legal where I would be out of my depth, like trademarking and copyrighting.

## What is BRF's role in this?

My theory is that God put this idea into BRF because it was the perfect organisation to help it grow, like the 'good ground' in the parable of the sower. BRF provides the aforementioned resources and office back-up that enable Jane, Martyn and me to get on with the face-to-face ministry. BRF gives us the space to talk about the ministry at a deeper level and understands how important people are to making things work well. It isn't 'owned' by any particular denomination but is respected by a wide spectrum of denominations, so we can happily work alongside most Christian churches. It also has a faithful foundation of praying friends: in the Messy Church growth, we're reaping the hours, days, weeks and years you've spent committing BRF and its ministry to God.

## What do the next ten years look like?

Of course we have no idea! If you'd asked us this question ten years ago, we wouldn't have dared dream of anything like the reality. I'll be even wrinklier in another ten, so I hope we'll have found funding to bring some young, lively, wise people on to the BRF team to keep us in touch with the ongoing needs of families and young people. There will probably be continued numerical growth—maybe up to 4000 Messy Churches by 2024—but this must flatten out eventually. I think we'll have a whole range of tried-and-tested resources for helping families move on in faith. I hope we'll have found great ways of helping older children and teenagers stay on board as leaders. Probably the established church will be taking us seriously if we've survived that long, so there should be many more paid professionals working full-time in Messy Churches. I'd like to think we'd have full-time coordinators in several countries across the world, too. In ten years, there could be two generations of families who have grown up thinking that Messy Church is the norm rather than the exception to the rule, so it will have evolved naturally to meet their (for now) unimaginable needs and to make the most of the (for now) unimaginable technology.

## How can BRF supporters be part of this development?

Please continue to pray, to keep that good ground well fertilised. Help us to find ways of putting the ministry on a more secure financial footing: to survive the next decade, we must be less reliant on the very few *very* generous people who currently fund us: we need a broader base of individuals and churches giving a little regularly. Do keep being proud of us: we love being part of the BRF family and are always very touched when any of you take the trouble to tell friends about our work or to encourage us personally with a letter or email. Thank you for all you do.

# Ten reasons to go on retreat

*Daniel Muñoz*

In his 2012 book *Falling Upward*, the American Franciscan Richard Rohr explores spirituality from the perspective of 'the two halves of life'. The first half is what he describes as the time of learning, focusing on the outer world and developing our own personal identity. The second half is the time of unlearning, focusing on the inner world and reconnecting with God in deeper, more transformational ways. In fact, he says, this latter dimension of the second half of life stands at the heart of religion (in Latin, *re-ligio*, meaning 'reconnect').

In my experience as a priest, first in parish ministry and now as chaplain of Los Olivos retreat centre in Spain, whether we find ourselves in the first or the second half of life, our deepest human need is to reconnect with ourselves, with God and with the world around us in ways that are life-giving. I have seen this, especially, in the many people who have come to Los Olivos over the last few years. So, although the reasons why people come on retreat are very varied, most share a similar experience of reconnecting with God, oneself and others in new ways.

Now, a personal confession. I am not a great believer in anything that sells itself as 'ten (or any other number) easy steps' to lose weight, find love, be successful in life, or whatever. In fact, whenever I read articles advocating easy recipes or steps to change my life, my first reaction is one of scepticism and suspicion. Because this article gives you ten reasons for going on retreat, a word of warning is required. These are not the top ten reasons why retreats are great and can change your life. Nor is it an exhaustive list to sum up all that a retreat can offer. Instead, these are just some of the most recurring themes, motivations and benefits that those who have come on retreat to Los Olivos have shared with us. I pray you will find them helpful.

- Connecting with your inner self: Retreats offer you a safe space to look inside and do some necessary inner work. This can be done through times of silence, personal reflection, guided meditation and prayerful exercises. A good retreat will enable you to reconnect with your inner self and to create space for God to reconnect with you.

- Recharging your batteries: Retreat times are not just beneficial for our spiritual life. They are opportunities to be physically, mentally and spiritually refreshed. Most retreats will provide a balance of times of personal prayer and corporate worship, times to be spiritually encouraged and intellectually stimulated, times to share in conversation and enjoy good healthy food, times to rest and times to engage in activity. A good retreat should be a life-giving holistic experience.

- Focusing on God: In the midst of the busyness of life, we tend to compartmentalise the different aspects of our lives, our spiritual life becoming one of the many things we 'do'. Our times of personal prayer and Bible meditation tend to be squeezed into a few minutes at the beginning or end of the day. Retreat times can help you reconnect with God by opening all of your senses to God's presence and activity within you and around you. This often leads to transformation and a renewed commitment to focus on God in more intentional ways in your daily life.

- Spiritual formation and transformation: At the heart of the Way of Jesus is the invitation to become like little children and unlearn things we have come to take for granted, in order to learn afresh what it means to be fully human, to be a follower of the Rabbi of Nazareth and to deepen our relationship with God and others. Retreats are crucial in this ongoing process of spiritual formation, providing a space in which your spiritual muscles can be stretched and strengthened for the journey ahead. They also provide the content, through themed, 'taught' retreats and courses, to feed you spiritually and intellectually.

- Space to reflect: There are times when we experience big changes in our personal circumstances, whether they relate to family, other relationships or professional life. These are times in which we have more questions than answers. When you find yourself at a crossroad in life and need some distance from it all to make sense of difficult situations or discern the way forward, a retreat will provide space to think, reflect and clarify your thoughts. It can become a time where healing happens, or when you gain new insights into God's will for your life.

- Being in community: One of the most exciting aspects of going on retreat is to be part of a community of people for a few days. At Los Olivos, we have discovered that being community—eating, praying, talking, learning, laughing and sharing our hopes and fears together—

is central to the experience of hospitality. One of the most rewarding experiences in this type of ministry is when a group of ten or twelve or 15 individuals who have never met before come together at the beginning of a week, and, by the end of the week, are no longer a group of individuals but have become a community. They are no longer strangers to each other; they have become friends.

- Doing something you've never done before: Retreats are opportunities to try new things. They could include exploring a new dimension of Christian spirituality, getting creative and having a go at painting, sculpting or cooking exotic food, having a massage, or simply exploring a new area of the country or the world.

- Space to be: Retreat times provide a conducive environment to 'be', and not just 'do'—to *be* in the present moment, aware of God's presence, without distractions and deadlines. This can be a difficult aspect of being on retreat, but equally it is a very liberating one.

- Mentoring and guidance: Most retreat houses offer opportunities to meet with a spiritual director or companion, to share your journey and help you discern where God is, or what God might be saying to you at that given time. Even if you already have a spiritual director back home, meeting with a different one can be a very useful exercise.

- Connecting with nature: Enjoying God's creation is central to many retreat centres. Los Olivos is in the heart of the Sierra Nevada National Park in southern Spain, with many opportunities for mountain walks, bird watching, flower spotting and contemplating God's work through creation. This is true of many retreat centres around the world, where the location, often in a place of outstanding natural beauty, acts as a wonderful backdrop to the retreat itself.

So, whether you are a frequent retreat flier or someone who has never embarked on such a spiritual flight, I hope these ten reasons will encourage you to take time out to reconnect with yourself, with others and with God, through the precious gift of a personal retreat.

*Daniel Muñoz is chaplain to the Los Olivos retreat centre in the heart of the Sierra Nevada National Park in Spain. For details of Los Olivos, visit www.haciendalosolivos.org. For details of our BRF Quiet Days, visit brfonline.org.uk/events-and-quiet-days or contact BRF on 01865 319700.*

Daniel has also written Transformed by the Beloved: A guide to spiritual formation with St John of the Cross. *To order a copy, please see the order form on page 155, or visit www.brfonline.org.uk.*

# Recommended reading

*Kevin Ball*

**Why read books? For enjoyment, to be challenged, to learn, to discover?** *The Huffington Post*, **a US online newspaper, has published some unconventional reasons why you should be reading books.**

- Reading can help you relax and sleep better.
- It can keep your brain sharp into old age and may even stave off Alzheimer's.
- Self-help books can ease depression.
- Reading books that engage your emotions can boost your empathy and can even help you cultivate the ability to read the thoughts and feelings of others.

Whatever you think of this list, the survey that BRF ran last year revealed that, for you, reading Christian books is all about helping you to go deeper with your faith. So what books can BRF offer you right now, to help you stay sharp, empathetic and growing?

This year's Advent book is *Longing, Waiting, Believing* by Rodney Holder. Rodney's *New Daylight* notes on 'Our Creator God' in 2012 brought a refreshing look at the positive engagement of contemporary science with the biblical creation accounts. Rodney now brings his scientific insights to bear on the themes of Advent.

For many of us, prayer means speaking words already prepared on a service sheet, a hasty request when life presses in, or saying 'Amen' to someone else's words. But shouldn't prayer be far more than that? To help you discover the 'more', Daniel Wolpert invites you to explore twelve ancient prayer practices in *Creating a Life with God*.

*Journalling the Bible* aims to help you past the roadblock faced by many of us—struggling to read the Bible. Author Corin Child guides you through 40 exercises to help you start journalling your insights from Bible passages and how they resonate with your faith experience.

You can find more detail about these books and others on the pages that follow and on our website, www.brfonline.org.uk. Keep reading!

## Longing, Waiting, Believing
### Reflections for Advent, Christmas and Epiphany
### Rodney Holder

In the excitement of preparing for Christmas, the traditionally penitential nature of Advent is often overlooked. In BRF's Advent book for 2014, scientist Rodney Holder takes readers from 1 December to 6 January, covering the well-known events of the nativity story while also showing the relevance of the Advent focus on the 'four last things'—death, judgment, heaven and hell—as part of the build-up to celebrating the incarnation. He draws on relevant insights from his years of work at the interface between science and faith. Material for group use is included in the book.

*pb, 978 1 84101 756 3, 192 pages, £7.99 (Also available for Kindle)*

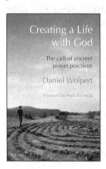

## Creating a Life with God
### The call of ancient prayer practices
### Daniel Wolpert

*Here was something that reached down into the core of our dilemma as human beings… something that struck a blow at the evil separating us from loving our brothers and sisters.*

Daniel Wolpert invites you to explore twelve ancient prayer practices that have been observed since records of humanity's search for God began. The prayer practices, which include the Jesus Prayer, apophatic prayer, *lectio divina*, body prayer, walking towards God, the examen, journalling and praying in nature, are explored with the help of travelling companions such as Ignatius Loyola, Julian of Norwich, Francis of Assisi and the anonymous author of *The Way of a Pilgrim*.

The journey to discover the true depth of prayer is not instant, warns Daniel, but it is of extreme importance for all who truly want to reach out and find God. *Creating a Life with God* also includes a step-by-step guide to the prayer practices and a model timetable for planning a quiet day or retreat using the book.

*pb, 978 0 85746 244 2, 192 pages, £7.99 (Also available for Kindle)*

## Journalling the Bible
### 40 creative writing exercises
### Corin Child

To grow in faith, becoming a better Christian, is the desire of many people, yet progress can remain elusive. Could the solution lie in writing things down—journalling?

Corin Child makes it easy to start journalling, by offering 40 exercises, arising from Bible passages across scripture. The hope is that by sensing the exhilaration of the biblical writers, you will be stirred to follow their example.

Each reflection is explored through reading the scripture passage and considering the passion of the text, illustrated in many cases by comparisons with other inspiring works, such as famous diaries, literature, songs, films or television programmes. It's then your turn to write, using the helpful journalling template as a guide.

*pb, 978 1 84101 736 5, 128 pages, £7.99 (Also available for Kindle)*

## Timothy Bear and the Baptism Box
### 12 five-minute stories and simple activities for baptism families
### Brian Sears

When his baby sister Teresa is baptised, Timothy Bear learns a lot about what baptism really means—and he discovers that some lessons are easier to learn than others!

*Timothy Bear and the Baptism Box* contains twelve easy-to-read stories, each exploring a different symbol or action found either in the Church of England baptism service or in the wider baptism journey. The stories lead to the creation of a child's own baptism box.

Baptism symbols and themes include water, oil, the lighted candle, repentance, forgiveness through the sacrifice of Jesus, the meaning of the Trinity, keeping promises, service, perseverance, becoming part of God's family and growing as a Christian. This is an ideal gift for 4–7s.

*pb, 978 0 85746 154 4, 96 pages, £6.99*

## Learning with Foundations21
### A seven-week course of study material
### Claire Musters

These two study resources, *Prayer* and *Jesus*, provide seven weeks of material for group or individual use. Each week includes an overview session with shorter follow-up sessions through the week, encouraging continuity between one meeting and the next, with questions and activities differentiated for different learning styles, and links to the BRF Foundations21 website (www.foundations21.net).

### Prayer
- Week 1: What is prayer?
- Week 2: Prayer in the Bible
- Week 3: Praying Jesus' way
- Week 4: Ways in to prayer
- Week 5: The discipline of prayer
- Week 6: The power of prayer
- Week 7: Praying with others

### Jesus
- Week 1: Jesus the Messiah
- Week 2: The divine nature of Jesus
- Week 3: Jesus' humanity
- Week 4: Jesus' teachings
- Week 5: Jesus' 'I am' sayings
- Week 6: Meeting with Jesus
- Week 7: Following Jesus

Prayer: *pb, 978 1 84101 695 5, 80 pages, £4.99*
Jesus: *pb, 978 1 84101 692 4, 80 pages, £4.99*

*Both titles are also available as PDF downloads.*

*To order copies of any of these books, please turn to the order form on page 155, or visit www.brfonline.org.uk.*

As a Christian charity, BRF is involved in seven distinct yet complementary areas.

- **BRF** (www.brf.org.uk) resources adults for their spiritual journey through Bible reading notes, books and Quiet Days. BRF also provides the infrastructure that supports our other specialist ministries.
- **Foundations21** (www.foundations21.net) provides flexible and innovative ways for individuals and groups to explore their Christian faith and discipleship through a multimedia internet-based resource.
- **Messy Church** (www.messychurch.org.uk), led by Lucy Moore, enables churches all over the UK (and increasingly abroad) to reach children and adults beyond the fringes of the church.
- **Barnabas in Churches** (www.barnabasinchurches.org.uk) helps churches to support, resource and develop their children's ministry with the under-11s more effectively.
- **Barnabas in Schools** (www.barnabasinschools.org.uk) enables primary school children and teachers to explore Christianity creatively and bring the Bible alive within RE and Collective Worship.
- **Faith in Homes** (www.faithinhomes.org.uk) supports families to explore and live out the Christian faith at home.
- **Who Let The Dads Out** (www.wholetthedadsout.org) inspires churches to engage with dads and their pre-school children.

At the heart of BRF's ministry is a desire to equip adults and children for Christian living—helping them to read and understand the Bible, explore prayer and grow as disciples of Jesus. We need your help to make an impact on the local church, local schools and the wider community.

- You could support BRF's ministry with a one-off gift or regular donation (using the response form on page 153).
- You could consider making a bequest to BRF in your will.
- You could encourage your church to support BRF as part of your church's giving to home mission—perhaps focusing on a specific area of our ministry, or a particular member of our Barnabas team.
- Most important of all, you could support BRF with your prayers.

If you would like to discuss how a specific gift or bequest could be used in the development of our ministry, please phone 01865 319700 or email enquiries@brf.org.uk.

**Whatever you can do or give, we thank you for your support.**

BRF has been helping individuals connect with the Bible for over 90 years. We want to support churches as they seek to encourage church members into regular Bible reading.

## Order a Bible reading resources pack

This pack is designed to give your church the tools to publicise our Bible reading notes. It includes:

- Sample Bible reading notes for your congregation to try.
- Publicity resources, including a poster.
- A church magazine feature about Bible reading notes.

The pack is free, but we welcome a £5 donation to cover the cost of postage. If you require a pack to be sent outside the UK or require a specific number of sample Bible reading notes, please contact us for postage costs. More information about what the current pack contains is available on our website.

## How to order and find out more

- Visit www.biblereadingnotes.org.uk/for-churches/
- Telephone BRF on 01865 319700 between 9.15 am and 5.30 pm.
- Write to us at BRF, 15 The Chambers, Vineyard, Abingdon, OX14 3FE

## Keep informed about our latest initiatives

We are continuing to develop resources to help churches encourage people into regular Bible reading, wherever they are on their journey. Join our email list at www.biblereadingnotes.org.uk/helpingchurches/ to stay informed about the latest initiatives that your church could benefit from.

## Introduce a friend to our notes

We can send information about our notes and current prices for you to pass on. Please contact us.

BRF is a Registered Charity

# BRF MINISTRY APPEAL RESPONSE FORM

I want to help BRF by funding some of its core ministries. Please use my gift for:
❑ Where most needed  ❑ Barnabas Children's Ministry  ❑ Foundations21
❑ Messy Church  ❑ Who Let The Dads Out?
Please complete all relevant sections of this form and print clearly.

Title _____ First name/initials _____ Surname _____
Address _____
_____ Postcode _____
Telephone _____ Email _____

## Regular giving
If you would like to give by direct debit, please tick the box below and fill in details:

❑ I would like to make a regular gift of £ _____ per month / quarter / year
*(delete as appropriate)* by Direct Debit. (Please complete the form on page 159.)

If you would like to give by standing order, please contact Debra McKnight (tel: 01865 319700; email debra.mcknight@brf.org.uk; write to BRF address).

## One-off donation
Please accept my special gift of
❑ £10  ❑ £50  ❑ £100  (other) £ _____  by

❑ Cheque / Charity Voucher payable to 'BRF'
❑ Visa / Mastercard / Charity Card
*(delete as appropriate)*

Name on card _____

Card no. [ ][ ][ ][ ][ ] [ ][ ][ ][ ][ ] [ ][ ][ ][ ][ ] [ ][ ][ ][ ][ ]

Start date [ ][ ] [ ][ ]    Expiry date [ ][ ] [ ][ ]

Security code [ ][ ][ ]

Signature _____ Date _____

❑ I would like to give a legacy to BRF. Please send me further information.

❑ I want BRF to claim back tax on this gift.
**(If you tick this box, please fill in gift aid declaration overleaf.)**

**Please detach and send this completed form to:** BRF, 15 The Chambers, Vineyard, Abingdon OX14 3FE.          BRF is a Registered Charity (No.233280)

# GIFT AID DECLARATION

## Bible Reading Fellowship

Please treat as Gift Aid donations all qualifying gifts of money made
today ☐    in the past 4 years ☐    in the future ☐    (tick all that apply)

I confirm I have paid or will pay an amount of Income Tax and/or Capital Gains Tax for each tax year (6 April to 5 April) that is at least equal to the amount of tax that all the charities that I donate to will reclaim on my gifts for that tax year. I understand that other taxes such as VAT or Council Tax do not qualify. I understand the charity will reclaim 25p of tax on every £1 that I give.

☐    My donation does not qualify for Gift Aid.


Signature _____

Date _____

**Notes:**

1. Please notify BRF if you want to cancel this declaration, change your name or home address, or no longer pay sufficient tax on your income and/or capital gains.

2. If you pay Income Tax at the higher/additional rate and want to receive the additional tax relief due to you, you must include all your Gift Aid donations on your Self-Assessment tax return or ask HM Revenue and Customs to adjust your tax code.

GL0314

## BRF PUBLICATIONS ORDER FORM

Please send me the following book(s):

| | | Quantity | Price | Total |
|---|---|---|---|---|
| 756 3 | Longing, Waiting, Believing (R. Holder) | | £7.99 | |
| 688 7 | Creative Prayer Ideas (C. Daniel) | | £8.99 | |
| 651 1 | Mary (A. Jones) | | £8.99 | |
| 736 5 | Journalling the Bible (C. Child) | | £7.99 | |
| 244 2 | Creating a Life with God (D. Wolpert) | | £7.99 | |
| 584 2 | Transformed by the Beloved (D. Muñoz) | | £6.99 | |
| 154 4 | Timothy Bear and the Baptism Box (B. Sears) | | £6.99 | |
| 695 5 | Prayer (C. Musters) | | £4.99 | |
| 692 4 | Jesus (C. Musters) | | £4.99 | |

Total cost of books £ _____
Donation £ _____
Postage and packing £ _____
TOTAL £ _____

| POSTAGE AND PACKING CHARGES | | | | |
|---|---|---|---|---|
| order value | UK | Europe | Surface | Air Mail |
| £7.00 & under | £1.25 | £3.00 | £3.50 | £5.50 |
| £7.01–£30.00 | £2.25 | £5.50 | £6.50 | £10.00 |
| Over £30.00 | free | prices on request | | |

Please complete the payment details below and send with payment to: **BRF, 15 The Chambers, Vineyard, Abingdon OX14 3FE**

Name _____

Address _____

_____ Postcode _____

Tel _____ Email _____

Total enclosed £ _____ (cheques should be made payable to 'BRF')

**Please charge my** Visa ❏ Mastercard ❏ with £ _____

Card no: [ ][ ][ ][ ][ ][ ][ ][ ][ ][ ][ ][ ][ ][ ][ ][ ]

Expires [ ][ ][ ][ ] Security code [ ][ ][ ]

Signature (essential if paying by card) _____

## GUIDELINES INDIVIDUAL SUBSCRIPTIONS

❏ I would like to take out a subscription myself:

Your name _____

Your address _____

_____

_____ Postcode _____

Tel _____ Email _____

Please send *Guidelines* beginning with the January 2015 / May 2015 /
September 2015 issue: (delete as applicable)

| (please tick box) | UK | SURFACE | AIR MAIL |
|---|---|---|---|
| GUIDELINES | ❏ £15.99 | ❏ £23.25 | ❏ £25.50 |
| GUIDELINES 3-year sub | ❏ £40.50 | | |
| GUIDELINES PDF download | ❏ £12.75 (UK and overseas) | | |

Please complete the payment details below and send with appropriate
payment to: **BRF, 15 The Chambers, Vineyard, Abingdon OX14 3FE**

Total enclosed £ _____ (cheques should be made payable to 'BRF')

**Please charge my** Visa ❏   Mastercard ❏   with £ _____

Card no: ☐☐☐☐☐☐☐☐☐☐☐☐☐☐☐☐☐☐☐

Expires ☐☐☐   Security code ☐☐☐

Signature (essential if paying by card) _____

To set up a direct debit, please also complete the form on page 159 and send
it to BRF with this form.

BRF is a Registered Charity

## GUIDELINES GIFT SUBSCRIPTIONS

❏ I would like to give a gift subscription (please provide both names and addresses:

Your name _____

Your address _____

_____ Postcode _____

Tel _____ Email _____

Gift subscription name _____

Gift subscription address _____

_____ Postcode _____

Gift message (20 words max. or include your own gift card for the recipient)

_____

_____

Please send *Guidelines* beginning with the January 2015 / May 2015 / September 2015 issue: (delete as applicable)

| (please tick box) | UK | SURFACE | AIR MAIL |
|---|---|---|---|
| GUIDELINES | ❏ £15.99 | ❏ £23.25 | ❏ £25.50 |
| GUIDELINES 3-year sub | ❏ £40.50 | | |
| GUIDELINES PDF download | ❏ £12.75 (UK and overseas) | | |

Please complete the payment details below and send with appropriate payment to: **BRF, 15 The Chambers, Vineyard, Abingdon OX14 3FE**

Total enclosed £ _____ (cheques should be made payable to 'BRF')

**Please charge my** Visa ❏ Mastercard ❏ with £ _____

Card no: | | | | | | | | | | | | | | | | | | |

Expires | | | | Security code | | |

Signature (essential if paying by card) _____

To set up a direct debit, please also complete the form on page 159 and send it to BRF with this form.

# DIRECT DEBIT PAYMENTS

Now you can pay for your annual subscription to BRF notes using Direct Debit. You need only give your bank details once, and the payment is made automatically every year until you cancel it. If you would like to pay by Direct Debit, please use the form opposite, entering your BRF account number under 'Reference'.

You are fully covered by the Direct Debit Guarantee:

---

## The Direct Debit Guarantee

- This Guarantee is offered by all banks and building societies that accept instructions to pay Direct Debits.
- If there are any changes to the amount, date or frequency of your Direct Debit, The Bible Reading Fellowship will notify you 10 working days in advance of your account being debited or as otherwise agreed. If you request The Bible Reading Fellowship to collect a payment, confirmation of the amount and date will be given to you at the time of the request.
- If an error is made in the payment of your Direct Debit, by The Bible Reading Fellowship or your bank or building society, you are entitled to a full and immediate refund of the amount paid from your bank or building society.
  - – If you receive a refund you are not entitled to, you must pay it back when The Bible Reading Fellowship asks you to.
- You can cancel a Direct Debit at any time by simply contacting your bank or building society. Written confirmation may be required. Please also notify us.

---

The Bible Reading Fellowship

## Instruction to your bank or building society to pay by Direct Debit

Please fill in the whole form using a ballpoint pen and send to The Bible Reading Fellowship, 15 The Chambers, Vineyard, Abingdon OX14 3FE.

Service User Number:

| 5 | 5 | 8 | 2 | 2 | 9 |
|---|---|---|---|---|---|

### Name and full postal address of your bank or building society

| To: The Manager | Bank/Building Society |
|---|---|
| Address | |
| | |
| | |
| | Postcode |

### Name(s) of account holder(s)

| |
|---|

### Branch sort code

| | | | | | |
|---|---|---|---|---|---|

### Bank/Building Society account number

| | | | | | | | |
|---|---|---|---|---|---|---|---|

### Reference

| | | | | | | |
|---|---|---|---|---|---|---|

### Instruction to your Bank/Building Society

Please pay The Bible Reading Fellowship Direct Debits from the account detailed in this instruction, subject to the safeguards assured by the Direct Debit Guarantee.
I understand that this instruction may remain with The Bible Reading Fellowship and, if so, details will be passed electronically to my bank/building society.

| Signature(s) | |
|---|---|
| | |
| Date | |

Banks and Building Societies may not accept Direct Debit instructions for some types of account.

This page is intentionally left blank.